GREAT SPEECHES

GREAT

SPEECHES

VIKING
an imprint of
PENGUIN BOOKS

VIKING

Published by the Penguin Group
Penguin Group (Australia)
250 Camberwell Road, Camberwell, Victoria 3124, Australia
(a division of Pearson Australia Group Pty Ltd)
Penguin Group (USA) Inc.
375 Hudson Street, New York, New York 10014, USA
Penguin Group (Canada)
10 Alcorn Avenue, Toronto, Ontario, Canada M4V 3B2
(a division of Pearson Penguin Canada Inc.)
Penguin Books Ltd
80 Strand, London WC2R 0RL, England
Penguin Ireland
25 St Stephen's Green, Dublin 2, Ireland
(a division of Penguin Books Ltd)
Penguin Books India Pvt Ltd
11 Community Centre, Panchsheel Park, New Delhi – 110 017, India
Penguin Group (NZ)
67 Apollo Drive, Mairangi Bay, Auckland 1310, New Zealand
(a division of Pearson New Zealand Ltd)
Penguin Books (South Africa) (Pty) Ltd
24 Sturdee Avenue, Rosebank, Johannesburg 2196, South Africa

Penguin Books Ltd, Registered Offices: 80 Strand, London, WC2R 0RL, England

First published by Penguin Group (Australia),
a division of Pearson Australia Group Pty Ltd, 2005

10 9 8 7 6 5 4 3

Text selection copyright © Penguin Group (Australia) 2005

The moral right of the authors has been asserted

Cover and text design by Adam Laszczuk © Penguin Group
Typeset in Perpetua by Post Pre-press Group, Queensland
Printed in China by Bookbuilders

National Library of Australia
Cataloguing-in-Publication data:

Great speeches.

ISBN 13: 978 0 670 02883 2
ISBN 10: 0 670 02883 5

1. Speeches, addresses, etc. I. Title.

080

www.penguin.com.au

CONTENTS

SPEECHES FROM EARLIER TIMES

MEMORIALS, FAREWELLS
& PATRIOTIC SPEECHES

SPEECHES OF WAR & REVOLUTION

POLITICAL SPEECHES

INSPIRATIONAL SPEECHES

AUSTRALIAN SPEECHES

LITERARY SPEECHES

SPEECHES FROM

EARLIER TIMES

PERICLES (495–429 BC)

The renowned Athenian statesman, Pericles, delivered his
funeral oration in 431 BC in memorial of those killed
during the battle of the Peloponnesian War. While praising
the virtue of Greece's fallen sons, he extolled the value
of democratic government.

Many of those who have spoken before me on these
occasions have commended the author of that law which
we now are obeying for having instituted an oration to the
honor of those who sacrifice their lives in fighting for their
country. For my part, I think it sufficient for men who have
proved their virtue in action, by action to be honored for
it – by such as you see the public gratitude now performing
about this funeral; and that the virtues of many ought not to be
endangered by the management of any one person when their
credit must precariously depend on his oration, which may
be good and may be bad. Difficult, indeed, it is, judiciously
to handle a subject where even probable truth will hardly
gain assent. The hearer, enlightened by a long acquaintance,
and warm in his affection, may quickly pronounce everything unfavorably expressed in respect to what he wishes and
what he knows – while the stranger pronounces all exaggerated through envy of those deeds which he is conscious are
above his own achievement. For the praises bestowed upon
others are then only to be endured, when men imagine they
can do those feats they hear to have been done; they envy
what they cannot equal, and immediately pronounce it false.
Yet, as this solemnity hath received its sanction from the
authority of our ancestors, it is my duty also to obey the law

and to endeavor to procure, as far as I am able, the good-will and approbation of all my audience.

I shall therefore begin first with our forefathers, since both justice and decency require we should on this occasion bestow on them an honorable remembrance. In this our country they kept themselves always firmly settled, and through their valor handed it down free to every since-succeeding generation. Worthy, indeed, of praise are they, and yet more worthy are our immediate fathers, since, enlarging their own inheritance into the extensive empire which we now possess, they bequeathed that, their work of toil, to us their sons. Yet even these successes we ourselves here present, we who are yet in the strength and vigor of our days, have nobly improved, and have made such provisions for this our Athens that now it is all-sufficient in itself to answer every exigence of war and of peace. I mean not here to recite those martial exploits by which these ends were accomplished, or the resolute defenses we ourselves and our fathers have made against the formidable invasions of Barbarians and Greeks – your own knowledge of these will excuse the long detail. But by what methods we have risen to this height of glory and power, by what polity and by what conduct we are thus aggrandized, I shall first endeavor to show, and then proceed to the praise of the deceased. These, in my opinion, can be no impertinent topics on this occasion; thus discussion of them must be beneficial to this numerous company of Athenians and of strangers.

We are happy in a form of government which cannot envy the laws of our neighbors – for it hath served as a model to others, but is original at Athens. And this our form, as committed not to the few, but to the whole body of the people, is called a democracy. How different soever in a private capacity, we all enjoy the same general equality our laws are fitted to preserve; and superior honors just as we excel. The public administration is not confined to a particular family, but is attainable only by merit. Poverty is not a hindrance, since whoever is able to serve his country meets with no obstacle to preferment from his first obscurity. The offices of the state we go through without obstructions from one another; and live together in the mutual endearments of private life without suspicions; not angry with a neighbor for following the bent of his own humor, nor putting on that countenance of discontent, which pains though it cannot punish – so that in private life we converse without diffidence of damage, while we dare not on any account offend against the public, through the reverence we bear to the magistrates and the laws, chiefly to those enacted for redress of the injured, and to those unwritten, a breach of which is thought a disgrace. Our laws have further provided for the mind most frequent intermissions of care by the appointment of public recreations and sacrifices throughout the year, elegantly performed with a peculiar pomp, the daily delight of which is a charm that puts melancholy to flight. The grandeur of this our Athens causeth the produce of the whole earth to be imported here, by which we reap a familiar enjoyment, not more of the delicacies of our own growth than of those of other nations.

In the affairs of war we excel those of our enemies, who adhere to methods opposite to our own. For we lay open Athens to general resort, nor ever drive any stranger from us whom either improvement or curiosity hath brought amongst us, lest any enemy should hurt us by seeing what is never concealed. We place not so great a confidence in the preparatives and artifices of war as in the native warmth of our souls impelling us to action. In point of education the youth of some peoples are inured, by a course of laborious exercise, to support toil and exercise like men, but we, notwithstanding our easy and elegant way of life, face all the dangers of war as intrepidly as they. This may be proved by facts, since the Lacedæmonians never invade our territories barely with their own, but with the united strength of all their confederates. But when we invade the dominions of our neighbors, for the most part we conquer without difficulty in an enemy's country those who fight in defense of their own habitations. The strength of our whole force no enemy yet hath ever experienced, because it is divided by our naval expeditions, or engaged in the different quarters of our service by land. But if anywhere they engage and defeat a small party of our forces, they boastingly give it out a total defeat; and if they are beat, they were certainly overpowered by our united strength. What though from a state of inactivity rather than to laborious exercise, or with a natural rather than an acquired valor, we learn to encounter danger? – this good, at least, we receive from it, that we never droop under the apprehension of possible misfortunes, and when we hazard the danger, are found no less courageous than those who are continually inured to it. In these respects our whole community deserves justly to be admired, and in many we have yet to mention.

In our manner of living we show an elegance tempered with frugality, and we cultivate philosophy without enervating

the mind. We display our wealth in the season of beneficence, and not in the vanity of discourse. A confession
of poverty is disgrace to no man, no effort to avoid it is
disgrace indeed. There is visible in the same persons an
attention to their own private concerns and those of the
public; and in others engaged in the labors of life there is
a competent skill in the affairs of government. For we are
the only people who think him that does not meddle in
state affairs – not indolent, but good for nothing. And yet
we pass the soundest judgements, and are quick at catching
the right apprehensions of things, not thinking that words
are prejudicial to actions, but rather the not being duly prepared by previous debate before we are obliged to proceed
to execution. Herein consists our distinguishing excellence,
that in the hour of action we show the greatest courage,
and yet debate beforehand the expediency of our measures.
The courage of others is the result of ignorance; delibera-
tion makes them cowards. And those undoubtedly must be
owned to have the greatest souls, who, most acutely sensible of the miseries of war and the sweets of peace, are not
hence in the least deterred from facing danger.

In acts of beneficence, further, we differ from the many.
We preserve friends not by receiving, but by conferring,
obligations. For he who does a kindness hath the advantage
over him who, by the law of gratitude, becomes a debtor
to his benefactor. The person obliged is compelled to act
the more insipid part, conscious that a return of kindness is
merely a payment and not an obligation. And we alone are
splendidly beneficent to others, not so much from inter-
ested motives as for the credit of pure liberality. I shall
sum up what yet remains by only adding that our Athens

in general is the school of Greece; and that every single Athenian amongst us is excellently formed, by his personal qualification, for all the various scenes of active life, acting with a most graceful demeanor and a most ready habit of despatch.

That I have not on this occasion made use of a pomp of words, but the truth of facts, that height to which by such a conduct this state hath risen, is an undeniable proof. For we are now the only people of the world who are found by experience to be greater than in report – the only people who, repelling the attacks of an invading enemy, exempt their defeat from the blush of indignation, and to their tributaries yield no discontent, as if subject to men unworthy to command. That we deserve our power, we need no evidence to manifest. We have great and signal proofs of this, which entitle us to the admiration of the present and future ages. We want no Homer to be the herald of our praise; no poet to deck off a history with the charms of verse, where the opinion of exploits must suffer by a strict relation. Every sea hath been opened by our fleets, and every land hath been penetrated by our armies, which have everywhere left behind them eternal monuments of our enmity and our friendship.

In the just defense of such a state, these victims of their own valor, scorning the ruin threatened to it, have valiantly fought and bravely died. And every one of those who survive is ready, I am persuaded, to sacrifice life in such a cause. And for this reason have I enlarged so much on national points, to give the clearest proof that in the present war we have more at stake than men whose public advantages are not so valuable, and to illustrate, by actual evidence, how great a commendation is due to them who are now my subject, and the greatest part of which they have already received. For the encomiums with which I have celebrated the state have been earned for it by the bravery of these and of men like these. And such compliments might be thought too high and exaggerated if passed on any Greeks but them alone. The fatal period to which these gallant souls are now reduced is the surest evidence of their merit – an evidence begun in their lives and completed in their deaths. For it is a debt of justice to pay superior honors to men who have devoted their lives in fighting for their country, though inferior to others in every virtue but that of valor. Their last service effaceth all former demerits – it extends to the public; their private demeanors reached only to a few. Yet not one of these was at all induced to shrink from danger, through fondness of those delights which the peaceful affluent life bestows – not one was the less lavish of his life, through that flattering hope attendant upon want, that poverty at length might be exchanged for affluence. One passion there was in their minds much stronger than these – the desire of vengeance on their enemies. Regarding this as the most honorable prize of dangers, they boldly rushed towards the mark to glut revenge and then to satisfy those secondary passions. The uncertain event they had already secured in hope; what their eyes showed plainly must be done they trusted their own valor to accomplish, thinking it more glorious to defend themselves and die in the attempt than to yield and live. From the reproach of cowardice, indeed, they fled, but presented their bodies to the shock of battle; when, insensible of fear, but triumphing in hope, in the doubtful charge they instantly dropped – and thus discharged the duty which brave men owed to their country.

As for you, who now survive them, it is your business to pray for a better fate, but to think it your duty also to preserve the same spirit and warmth of courage against your enemies; not judging of the expediency of this from a mere harangue – where any man indulging a flow of words may tell you what you yourselves know as well as he, how many advantages there are in fighting valiantly against your enemies – but, rather, making the daily-increasing grandeur of this community the object of your thoughts and growing quite enamored of it. And when it really appears great to your apprehensions, think again that this grandeur was acquired by brave and valiant men, by men who knew their duty, and in the moments of action were sensible of shame; who, whenever their attempts were unsuccessful, thought it no dishonor for their country to stand in need of anything their valor could do for it, and so made it the most glorious present. Bestowing thus their lives on the public, they have every one received a praise that will never decay, a sepulchre that will always be most illustrious – not that in which their bones lie moldering, but that in which their fame is preserved, to be on every occasion, when honor is the employ of either word or act, eternally remembered. For the whole earth is the sepulchre of illustrious men; nor is it the inscription on the columns in their native land alone that shows their merit, but the memorial of them, better than all inscriptions, in every foreign nation, reposited more durably in universal remembrance than on their own tombs. From this very moment, emulating these noble patterns, placing your happiness in liberty, and liberty in valor, be prepared to encounter all the dangers of war. For to be lavish of life is not so noble in those whom misfortunes have reduced to misery and despair, as in men who hazard the loss of a comfortable subsistence and the enjoyment of all the blessings this world affords by an unsuccessful enterprise. Adversity, after a series of ease and affluence, sinks deeper into the heart of a man of spirit than the stroke of death insensibly received in the vigor of life and public hope.

For this reason, the parents of those who are now gone, whoever of them may be attending here, I do not bewail — I shall rather comfort. It is well known to what unhappy accidents they were liable from the moment of their birth, and that happiness belongs to men who have reached the most glorious period of life, as these now have who are to you the source of sorrow — these whose life hath received its ample measure, happy in its continuance and equally happy in its conclusion. I know it in truth a difficult task to fix comfort in those breasts which will have frequent remembrances, in seeing the happiness of others, of what they once themselves enjoyed. And sorrow flows not from the absence of those good things we have never yet experienced, but from the loss of those to which we have been accustomed. They who are not yet by age past child-bearing should be comforted in the hope of having more. The children yet to be born will be a private benefit to some in causing them to forget such as no longer are, and will be a double benefit to their country in preventing its desolation and providing for its security. For those persons cannot in common justice be regarded as members of equal value to the public who have no children to expose to danger for its safety. But you, whose age is already far advanced, compute the greater share of happiness your longer time hath afforded for so much gain, persuaded in yourselves the remainder will be but short, and enlighten that space by the glory gained by these. It is greatness of soul alone that never grows old, nor is it wealth that delights in the latter stage of life, as some give out, so much as honor.

To you, the sons and brothers of the deceased, whatever number of you are here, a field of hardy contention is opened. For him who no longer is, every one is ready to commend, so that to whatever the height you push your deserts, you will scarce ever be thought to equal, but to be somewhat inferior to these. Envy will exert itself against a competitor while life remains; but when death stops the competition, affection will applaud without restraint.

If after this it be expected from me to say anything to you who are now reduced to a state of widowhood, about female virtue, I shall express it all in one short admonition: It is your greatest glory not to be deficient in the virtue peculiar to your sex, and to give men as little handle as possible to talk of your behavior, whether well or ill.

I have now discharged the province allotted me by the laws, and said what I thought most pertinent to this assembly. Our departed friends have by facts been already honored. Their children from this day till they arrive at manhood shall be educated at the public expense of the state which hath appointed so beneficial a meed for these and all future relics of the public contests. For wherever the greatest rewards are proposed for virtue, there the best of patriots are ever to be found. Now let every one respectively indulge in becoming grief for his departed friends, and then retire.

SOCRATES (469–399 BC)

The Greek philosopher Socrates sought to understand the meaning of concepts such as justice and courage, and encouraged others to think more deeply on such notions. He delivered this speech in 399 BC after he was accused of heresy and condemned to death.

For the sake of no long space of time, O Athenians, you will incur the character and reproach at the hands of those who wish to defame the city, of having put that wise man, Socrates, to death. For those who wish to defame you will assert that I am wise, though I am not. If, then, you had waited for a short time, this would have happened of its own accord; for observe my age, that it is far advanced in life, and near death. But I say this not to you all, but to those only who have condemned me to die. And I say this too to the same persons. Perhaps you think, O Athenians, that I have been convicted through the want of arguments, by which I might have persuaded you, had I thought it right to do and say anything so that I might escape punishment. Far otherwise: I have been convicted through want indeed, yet not of arguments, but of audacity and impudence, and of the inclination to say such things to you as would have been most agreeable for you to hear, and I lamented and bewailed and done and said many other things unworthy of me, as I affirm, but such as you are accustomed to hear from others.

But neither did I then think that I ought, for the sake of avoiding danger, to do anything unworthy of a freeman, nor do I now repent of having so defended myself; but I should much rather choose to die having so defended myself than to live in that way. For neither in a trial nor in battle is it right that I or any one else should employ every possible means whereby he may avoid death; for in battle it is frequently evident that a man might escape death by laying down his arms and throwing himself on the mercy of his pursuers. And there are many other devices in every danger, by which to avoid death, if a man dares to do and say everything.

But this is not difficult, O Athenians, to escape death, but it is much more difficult to avoid depravity, for it runs swifter than death. And now I, being slow and aged, am overtaken by the slower of the two; but my accusers, being strong and active, have been overtaken by the swifter, wickedness. And now I depart, condemned by you to death; but they condemned by truth, as guilty of iniquity and injustice: and I abide my sentence and so do they. These things, perhaps, ought so to be, and I think that they are for the best.

In the next place, I desire to predict to you who have condemned me, what will be your fate: for I am now in that condition in which men most frequently prophesy, namely, when they are about to die. I say then to you, O Athenians, who have condemned me to death, that immediately after my death a punishment will overtake you, far more severe, by Jupiter, than that which you have inflicted on me. For you have done this thinking you should be freed from the necessity of giving an account of your life. The very contrary however, as I affirm, will happen to you. Your accusers will be more numerous, whom I have now restrained, though you did not perceive it; and they will be more severe, inasmuch as they are younger and you will be more indignant. For, if you think that by putting men to death you will restrain any one from upbraiding you because you do not live well, you are much mistaken; for this method of escape is neither possible nor honorable, but that other is most honorable and most easy, not to put a check upon others, but for a man to take heed to himself, how he may be most perfect. Having predicted thus much to those of you who have condemned me, I take my leave of you.

But with you who have voted for my acquittal, I would gladly hold converse on what has now taken place, while the magistrates are busy and I am not yet carried to the place where I must die. Stay with me then, so long, O Athenians, for nothing hinders our conversing with each other, whilst we are permitted to do so; for I wish to make known to you, as being my friends, the meaning of that which has just now befallen me. To me then, O my judges, – and in calling you judges I call you rightly, – a strange thing has happened. For the wonted prophetic voice of my guardian deity, on every former occasion, even in the most trifling affairs, opposed me, if I was about to do anything wrong; but now, that has befallen me which ye yourselves behold, and which any one would think and which is supposed to be the extremity of evil, yet neither when I departed from home in the morning did the warning of the god oppose me, nor when I came up here to the place of trial, nor in my address when I was about to say anything; yet on other occasions it has frequently restrained me in the midst of speaking. But now it has never throughout this proceeding opposed me, either in what I did or said. What then do

I suppose to be the cause of this? I will tell you: what has befallen me appears to be a blessing; and it is impossible that we think rightly who suppose that death is an evil. A great proof of this to me is the fact that it is impossible but that the accustomed signal should have opposed me, unless I had been about to meet with some good.

Moreover, we may hence conclude that there is great hope that death is a blessing. For to die is one of two things: for either the dead may be annihilated and have no sensation of anything whatever; or, as it is said, there is a certain change and passage of the soul from one place to another. And if it is a privation of all sensations, as it were, a sleep in which the sleeper has no dream, death would be a wonderful gain. For I think that if anyone, having selected a night in which he slept so soundly as not to have had a dream, and having compared this night with all the other nights and days of his life, should be required on consideration to say how many days and nights he had passed better and more pleasantly than this night throughout his life, I think that not only a private person, but even a great king himself would find them easy to number in comparison with other days and nights. If, therefore, death is a thing of this kind, I say it is a gain; for thus all futurity appears to be nothing more than one night.

But if, on the other hand, death is a removal from hence to another place, and what is said be true, that all the dead are there, what greater blessing can there be than this, my judges? For if, on arriving at Hades, released from these who pretend to be judges, one shall find those who are true judges, and who are said to judge there, Minos and Rhadamanthus, Æacus and Triptolemus, and such others of the demigods as were just during their own life, would this be a sad removal? At what price would you not estimate a conference with Orpheus and Musæus, Hesiod and Homer? I indeed should be willing to die often, if this be true. For to me the sojourn there would be admirable, when I should meet with Palamedes, and Ajax, son of Telamon, and any other of the ancients who has died by an unjust sentence. The comparing my suffering with theirs would, I think, be no unpleasing occupation.

But the greatest pleasure would be to spend my time in questioning and examining the people there as I have done those here, and discovering who among them is wise, and who fancies himself to be so but is not. At what price, my judges, would not any one estimate the opportunity of questioning him who led that mighty army against Troy, or Ulysses, or Sisyphus, or ten thousand others, whom one might mention, both men and women, with whom to converse and associate, and to question them, would be an inconceivable happiness? Surely for that the judges there do not condemn to death; for in other respects those who live there are more happy than those that are here, and are henceforth immortal, if at least what is said be true.

You, therefore, O my judges, ought to entertain good hopes with respect to death, and to meditate on this one truth, that to a good man nothing is evil, neither while living nor when dead, nor are his concerns neglected by the gods. And what has befallen me is not the effect of chance; but this is clear to me, that now to die, and be freed from my cares, is better for me. On this account the warning in no way turned me aside; and I bear no resentment toward those who condemned me, or against my accusers, although they did not condemn and accuse me with this intention, but thinking to injure me: in this they deserve to be blamed.

This much, however, I beg of them. Punish my sons, when they grow up, O judges, paining them as I have pained you, if they appear to you to care for riches or anything else before virtue, and if they think themselves to be something when they are nothing, reproach them as I have done you, for not attending to what they ought, and for conceiving themselves to be something when they are worth nothing. If ye do this, both I and my sons shall have met with just treatment at your hands.

But it is now time to depart – for me to die, for you to live. But which of us is going to a better state is unknown to every one but God.

JOAN OF ARC (1412–1431)

At seventeen years of age, Joan of Arc lead French soldiers in numerous battles against English invaders, and her victories led to the crowning of Charles the VII. She was later accused of witchcraft and heresy, and sentenced to be burnt at the stake. She spoke these words at her trial in 1431.

Jean Delafontaine: 'When your Saints come to you, have they a light with them? Did you not see the light on a certain occasion when you heard the voices in the castle, without knowing if the voices were in your room?'

Joan of Arc: 'There is never a day that my Saints do not come to the castle; and they never come without light. And as to this voice of which you speak, I do not remember if on that occasion I saw the light or even Saint Catherine. I asked three things of my voices – my deliverance; that God would come to the help of the French, and protect the towns under their control; and the salvation of my soul.'

JA: (Addressing herself to the Judges) 'If it should be that I am taken to Paris, grant, I pray you, that I may have a copy of my questions and answers, so that I may lend them to those at Paris, and that I may be able to say to them: "Thus was I questioned at Rouen, and here are my answers." In this way, I shall not have to trouble again over so many questions.'

JD: 'You said that my Lord of Beauvais puts himself in great danger by bringing you to trial; of what danger were you speaking? In what peril or danger do we place ourselves – your Judges and the others?'

JA: 'I said to my Lord of Beauvais, "You say that you are my Judge; I do not know if you are, but take heed not to judge wrongly, because you would put yourself in great danger; and I warn you of it, so that, if Our Lord should punish you for it, I shall have done my duty in telling you."'

JD: 'But what is this peril or danger?'

JA: 'Saint Catherine has told me that I shall have help; I do not know if this will be to be delivered from prison, or if, whilst I am being tried, some disturbance may happen, by which I shall be delivered. The help will come to me, I think, in one way or the other. Besides this, my voices have told me that I shall be delivered by a great victory, and they add: "Be resigned, have no care for thy martyrdom, you will come in the end to the Kingdom of Paradise." They have told me this simply, absolutely, and without fail. What is meant by my martyrdom is the pain and adversity that I suffer in prison. I do not know if I shall have still greater suffering to bear; for that I refer me to God.'

JD: 'Since your voices told you that you would come in the end to the Kingdom of Paradise, have you felt assured of being saved and of not being damned in Hell?'

JA: 'I believe firmly what my voices have told me, that I shall be saved. I believe it as firmly as if I were already there.'

JD: 'After this revelation, do you believe that you cannot commit mortal sin?'

JA: 'I do not know, and in all things I wait on Our Lord.'

JD: 'That is an answer of great weight!'

JA: 'Yes, and one which I hold for a great treasure.'

Abraham Lincoln ❖ Great Speeches ❖ Napoleon Bonaparte ❖ Great Speeches ❖ Robert Emmet Great Speeches ❖ Napoleon Bonaparte ❖ Great Speeches ❖ Abraham Lincoln ❖ Great Speeches

MEMORIALS, FAREWELLS

Robert Emmet ❖ Great Speeches ❖ Napoleon Bonaparte ❖ Great Speeches ❖ Robert Emmet Great Speeches ❖ Abraham Lincoln ❖ Great

& PATRIOTIC SPEECHES

Speeches ❖ Napoleon Bonaparte ❖ Great Speeches Robert Emmet ❖ Great Speeches ❖ Abraham Lincoln ❖ Great Speeches ❖ Napoleon Bonaparte Great Speeches ❖ Robert Emmetn ❖ Great

ROBERT EMMET (1779–1803)

*An Irish rebel, Robert Emmet became the militant leader of
the United Irishmen. He was caught in 1803 after inciting
an unsuccessful uprising, and he made this speech from the
dock, having been sentenced to death for treason.*

My lords: — What have I to say why sentence of death
should not be pronounced on me according to law? I have
nothing to say that can alter your predetermination, nor
that it will become me to say with any view to the mitiga-
tion of that sentence which you are here to pronounce, and
I must abide by. But I have that to say which interests me
more than life, and which you have labored (as was necessarily your office in the present circumstances of this
oppressed country) to destroy. I have much to say why my
reputation should be rescued from the load of false accusa-
tion and calumny which has been heaped upon it. I do not
imagine that, seated where you are, your minds can be so
free from impurity as to receive the least impression from
what I am going to utter — I have no hopes that I can anchor
my character in the breast of a court constituted and tram-
meled as this is — I only wish, and it is the utmost I expect,
that your lordships may suffer it to float down your memo-
ries untainted by the foul breath of prejudice, until it finds
some more hospitable harbor to shelter it from the storm
by which it is at present buffeted.

Was I only to suffer death after being adjudged guilty by
your tribunal, I should bow in silence, and meet the fate that
awaits me without a murmur; but the sentence of law which
delivers my body to the executioner, will, through the

ministry of that law, labor in its own vindication to consign my character to obloquy – for there must be guilt somewhere: whether in the sentence of the court or in the catastrophe, posterity must determine. A man in my situation, my lords, has not only to encounter the difficulties of fortune, and the force of power over minds which it has corrupted or subjugated, but the difficulties of established prejudice: the man dies, but his memory lives. That mine may not perish, that it may live in the respect of my countrymen, I seize upon this opportunity to vindicate myself from some of the charges alleged against me. When my spirit shall be wafted to a more friendly port; when my shade shall have joined the bands of those martyred heroes who have shed their blood on the scaffold and in the field, in defense of their country and of virtue, this is my hope: I wish that my memory and name may animate those who survive me, while I look down with complacency on the destruction of that perfidious government which upholds its domination by blasphemy of the Most High – which displays its power over man as over the beasts of the forest – which sets man upon his brother, and lifts his hand in the name of God against the throat of his fellow who believes or doubts a little more or a little less than the government standard – a government which is steeled to barbarity by the cries of the orphans and the tears of the widows which it has made. (Interruption by the court.)

I appeal to the immaculate God – I swear by the throne of Heaven, before which I must shortly appear – by the blood of the murdered patriots who have gone before me – that my conduct has been through all this peril and all my purposes, governed only by the convictions which

I have uttered, and by no other view, than that of their cure, and the emancipation of my country from the super-inhuman oppression under which she has so long and too patiently travailed; and that I confidently and assuredly hope that, wild and chimerical as it may appear, there is still union and strength in Ireland to accomplish this noble enterprise. Of this I speak with the confidence of intimate knowledge, and with the consolation that appertains to that confidence. Think not, my lords, I say this for the petty gratification of giving you a transitory uneasiness; a man who never yet raised his voice to assert a lie, will not hazard his character with posterity by asserting a falsehood on a subject so important to his country, and on an occasion like this. Yes, my lords, a man who does not wish to have his epitaph written until his country is liberated, will not leave a weapon in the power of envy; nor a pretense to impeach the probity which he means to preserve even in the grave to which tyranny consigns him. (Interruption by the court.)

Again I say, that what I have spoken, was not intended for your lordship, whose situation I commiserate rather than envy – my expressions were for my countrymen; if there is a true Irishman present, let my last words cheer him in the hour of his affliction. (Interruption by the court.)

I have always understood it to be the duty of a judge when a prisoner has been convicted, to pronounce the sentence of the law; I have also understood that judges sometimes think it their duty to hear with patience, and to speak with humanity; to exhort the victim of the laws, and to offer with tender benignity his opinions of the motives by which he was actuated in the crime, of which he had been adjudged guilty: that a judge has thought it his duty so to have done, I have no doubt – but where is the boasted freedom of your institutions, where is the vaunted impartiality, clemency, and mildness of your courts of justice, if an unfortunate prisoner, whom your policy, and not pure justice, is about to deliver into the hands of the executioner, is not suffered to explain his motives sincerely and truly, and to vindicate the principles by which he was actuated?

My lords, it may be a part of the system of angry justice, to bow a man's mind by humiliation to the purposed ignominy of the scaffold; but worse to me than the purposed shame, or the scaffold's terrors, would be the shame of such unfounded imputations as have been laid against me in this court: you, my lord [Lord Norbury], are a judge, I am the supposed culprit; I am a man, you are a man also; by a revolution of power, we might change places, though we never could change characters; if I stand at the bar of this court, and dare not vindicate my character, what a farce is your justice? If I stand at this bar and dare not vindicate my character, how dare you calumniate it? Does the sentence of death which your unhallowed policy inflicts on my body, also condemn my tongue to silence and my reputation to reproach? Your executioner may abridge the period of my existence, but while I exist I shall not forbear to vindicate my character and motives from your aspersions; and as a man to whom fame is dearer than life, I will make the last use of that life in doing justice to that reputation which is to live after me, and which is the only legacy I can leave to those I honor and love, and for whom I am proud to perish. As men, my lord, we must appear at the great day at one common tribunal, and it will then remain for the searcher of all hearts to show a collective universe who was engaged in the most virtuous actions, or actuated by the purest motives – my country's oppressors or – (Interruption by the court.)

My lord, will a dying man be denied the legal privilege of exculpating himself, in the eyes of the community, of an undeserved reproach thrown upon him during his trial, by charging him with ambition, and attempting to cast away, for a paltry consideration, the liberties of his country? Why did your lordship insult me? or rather why insult justice, in demanding of me why sentence of death should not be pronounced? I know, my lord, that form prescribes that you should ask the question; the form also presumes a right of answering. This no doubt may be dispensed with – and so might the whole ceremony of trial, since sentence was already pronounced at the castle, before your jury was impaneled; your lordships are but the priests of the oracle, and I submit; but I insist on the whole of the forms.

I am charged with being an emissary of France! An emissary of France! And for what end? It is alleged that I wished to sell the independence of my country! And for what end? Was this the object of my ambition? And is this the mode by which a tribunal of justice reconciles contradictions? No, I am no emissary; and my ambition was to hold a place among the deliverers of my country – not in power, nor in profit, but in the glory of the achievement! Sell my country's independence to France! And for what? Was it for a change of masters? No! But for ambition! O my country, was it personal ambition that could influence me? Had it been the soul of my actions, could I not by my education and fortune, by the rank and consideration of my family, have placed myself among the proudest of my oppressors?

My country was my idol; to it I sacrificed every selfish, every endearing sentiment; and for it, I now offer up my life. O God! No, my lord; I acted as an Irishman, determined on delivering my country from the yoke of a foreign and unrelenting tyranny, and from the more galling yoke of a domestic faction, which is its joint partner and perpetrator in the parricide, for the ignominy of existing with an exterior of splendor and of conscious depravity. It was the wish of my heart to extricate my country from this doubly riveted despotism.

I wished to place her independence beyond the reach of any power on earth; I wished to exalt you to that proud station in the world.

Connection with France was indeed intended, but only as far as mutual interest would sanction or require. Were they to assume any authority inconsistent with the purest independence, it would be the signal for their destruction; we sought aid, and we sought it, as we had assurances we should obtain it – as auxiliaries in war and allies in peace.

Were the French to come as invaders or enemies, uninvited by the wishes of the people, I should oppose them to the utmost of my strength. Yes, my countrymen, I should advise you to meet them on the beach, with a sword in one hand, and a torch in the other; I would meet them with all the destructive fury of war; and I would animate my countrymen to immolate them in their boats, before they had contaminated the soil of my country. If they succeeded in landing, and if forced to retire before superior discipline, I would dispute every inch of ground, burn every blade of grass, and the last intrenchment of liberty should be my grave. What I could not do myself, if I should fall, I should leave as a last charge to my countrymen to accomplish; because I should feel conscious that life, any more than death, is unprofitable, when a foreign nation holds my country in subjection.

But it was not as an enemy that the succors of France were to land. I looked indeed for the assistance of France; but I wished to prove to France and to the world that Irishmen deserved to be assisted! — that they were indignant at slavery, and ready to assert the independence and liberty of their country.

I wished to procure for my country the guarantee which Washington procured for America. To procure an aid, which, by its example, would be as important as its valor, disciplined, gallant, pregnant with science and experience; which would perceive the good, and polish the rough points of our character. They would come to us as strangers, and leave us as friends, after sharing in our perils and elevating our destiny. These were my objects — not to receive new taskmasters, but to expel old tyrants; these were my views, and these only became Irishmen. It was for these ends I sought aid from France; because France, even as an enemy, could not be more implacable than the enemy already in the bosom of my country. (Interruption by the court.)

I have been charged with that importance in the efforts to emancipate my country, as to be considered the *key-stone* of the combination of Irishmen; or, as your lordship expressed it, 'the life and blood of conspiracy.' You do me honor overmuch. You have given to the subaltern all the credit of a superior. There are men engaged in this *conspiracy*, who are not only superior to me, but even to your own conceptions of yourself, my lord; men, before the splendor of whose genius and virtues, I should bow with respectful deference, and who would think themselves dishonored to be called your friend – who would not disgrace themselves by shaking your bloodstained hand – (Interruption by the court.)

What, my lord, shall you tell me, on the passage to that scaffold, which that tyranny, of which you are only the intermediary executioner, has erected for my murder, that I am accountable for all the blood that has and will be shed in this struggle of the oppressed against the oppressor? – shall you tell me this – and must I be so very a slave as not to repel it?

I do not fear to approach the omnipotent Judge, to answer for the conduct of my whole life; and am I to be appalled and falsified by a mere remnant of mortality here? By you, too, who, if it were possible to collect all the innocent blood that you have shed in your unhallowed ministry, in one great reservoir, your lordship might swim in it. (Interruption by the court.)

Let no man dare, when I am dead, to charge me with dishonor; let no man attaint my memory by believing that I could have engaged in any cause but that of my country's liberty and independence; or that I could have become the pliant minion of power in the oppression or the miseries of my countrymen. The proclamation of the provisional government speaks for our views; no inference can be tortured from it to countenance barbarity or debasement at home, or subjection, humiliation, or treachery from abroad; I would not have submitted to a foreign oppressor for the same reason that I would resist the foreign and domestic oppressor; in the dignity of freedom I would have fought upon the threshold of my country, and its enemy should enter only by passing over my lifeless corpse. Am I, who lived but for my country, and who have subjected myself to the dangers of the jealous and watchful oppressor, and the bondage of the grave, only to give my countrymen their rights, and my country her independence, and am I to be loaded with calumny, and not suffered to resent or repel it – no, God forbid!

If the spirits of the illustrious dead participate in the concerns and cares of those who are dear to them in this transitory life – oh, ever dear and venerated shade of my departed father, look down with scrutiny upon the conduct of your suffering son; and see if I have even for a moment deviated from those principles of morality and patriotism which it was your care to instil into my youthful mind, and for which I am now to offer up my life!

My lords, you are impatient for the sacrifice – the blood which you seek is not congealed by the artificial terrors which surround your victim; it circulates warmly and unruffled, through the channels which God created for noble purposes, but which you are bent to destroy, for purposes so grievous, that they cry to heaven. Be yet patient! I have but a few words more to say. I am going to my cold and silent grave: my lamp of life is nearly extinguished: my race is run: the grave opens to receive me, and I sink into its bosom! I have but one request to ask at my departure from this world – it is the charity of its silence! Let no man write my epitaph: for as no man who knows my motives dare now vindicate them, let not prejudice or ignorance asperse them. Let them and me repose in obscurity and peace, and my tomb remain uninscribed, until other times, and other men, can do justice to my character; when my country takes her place among the nations of the earth, then, and not till then, let my epitaph be written. I have done.

NAPOLEON BONAPARTE (1769–1821)

Napolean was a military genius, fearsome conqueror and gifted orator. He believed in taking care of his men, and instilled in them his own sense of destiny. This is his farewell speech to the old guard, after his failed invasion of Russia and defeat by the Allies in 1814.

Soldiers of my Old Guard: I bid you farewell. For twenty years I have constantly accompanied you on the road to honor and glory. In these latter times, as in the days of our prosperity, you have invariably been models of courage and fidelity. With men such as you our cause could not be lost; but the war would have been interminable; it would have been civil war, and that would have entailed deeper misfortunes on France.

I have sacrificed all my interests to those of the country.

I go, but you, my friends, will continue to serve France. Her happiness was my only thought. It will still be the object of my wishes. Do not regret my fate; if I have consented to survive, it is to serve your glory. I intend to write the history of the great achievements we have performed together. Adieu, my friends. Would I could press you all to my heart.

ABRAHAM LINCOLN (1809–1865)

*President of the United States from 1861 to 1865, Abraham
Lincoln fought to end slavery in America. In January 1863
he issued the Emancipation Proclamation which declared
those slaves within the Confederacy to be forever free. Later
that same year he delivered his legendary speech – the
Gettysburg Address.*

Four score and seven years ago our fathers brought forth
on this continent, a new nation, conceived in liberty, and
dedicated to the proposition that all men are created equal.

Now we are engaged in a great civil war, testing whether
that nation, or any nation so conceived and so dedicated,
can long endure. We are met on a great battlefield of that
war. We have come to dedicate a portion of that field, as a
final resting place for those who here gave their lives that
that nation might live. It is altogether fitting and proper
that we should do this.

But, in a larger sense, we cannot dedicate – we cannot
consecrate – we cannot hallow – this ground. The brave
men, living and dead, who struggled here, have consecrated
it, far above our poor power to add or detract. The world
will little note, nor long remember, what we say here, but
it can never forget what they did here. It is for us the living,
rather, to be dedicated here to the unfinished work which
they who fought here have thus far so nobly advanced. It is
rather for us to be here dedicated to the great task remaining before us – that from these honored dead we take
increased devotion to that cause for which they gave the
last full measure of devotion – that we here highly resolve

that these dead shall not have died in vain — that this nation, under God, shall have a new birth of freedom — and that government of the people, by the people, for the people, shall not perish from the earth.

SPEECHES OF

WAR & REVOLUTION

OLIVER CROMWELL (1599–1658)

*Son of a farmer and brewer, Oliver Cromwell grew up to lead
the rebellious forces against the armies of Charles I. Cromwell
gave this speech in 1655 at the dissolution of parliament,
after conquering Scotland and Ireland. He went on to form
a new parliament and proclaimed himself Lord Protector of
England.*

This government called you hither; the constitution thereof
being limited so – a single person and a Parliament. And
this was thought most agreeable to the general sense of the
nation;– having had experience enough by trial, of other
conclusions; judging this most likely to avoid the extremes
of monarchy on the one hand, and of democracy on the
other;– and yet not to found *dominium in gratia* 'either.'
And if so, then certainly to make the authority more than a
mere notion, it was requisite that it should be as it is in this
'frame of' government; which puts it upon a true and equal
balance. It has been already submitted to the judicious, true
and honest people of this nation, whether the balance be
not equal? And what their judgment is, is visible – by submission to it; by acting upon it; by restraining their trustees
from meddling with it. And it neither asks nor needs any
better ratification? But when trustees in Parliament shall,
by experience, find any evil in any parts of this 'frame of'
government, 'a question' referred by the government itself
to the consideration of the Protector and Parliament – of
which evil or evils time itself will be the best discoverer:–
how can it be reasonably imagined that a person or persons,
coming in by election, and standing under such obligations,

and so limited, and so necessitated by oath to govern for the people's good, and to make their love, under God, the best under-propping and only safe footing:– how can it, I say, be imagined that the present or succeeding Protectors will refuse to agree to alter any such thing in the government as may be found to be for the good of the people? Or to recede from anything which he might be convinced casts the balance too much to the single person? And although, for the present, the keeping up and having in his power the militia seems the hardest 'condition,' yet if the power of the militia should be yielded up at such a time as this, when there is as much need of it to keep this cause (now most evidently impugned by all enemies), as there was to get it 'for the sake of this cause':– what would become of us all! Or if it should not be equally placed in him and the Parliament, but yielded up at any time – it determines his power either for doing the good he ought, or hindering Parliaments from perpetuating themselves; from imposing what religion they please on the consciences of men, or what government they please upon the nation. Thereby subjecting us to dissettlement in every Parliament, and to the desperate consequences thereof. And if the nation shall happen to fall into a blessed peace, how easily and certainly will their charge be taken off, and their forces be disbanded! And then where will the danger be to have the militia thus stated? What if I should say: If there be a disproportion, or disequality as to the power, it is on the other hand!

And if this be so, wherein have you had cause to quarrel? What demonstrations have you held forth to settle me to your opinion? I would you had made me so happy as to have let me know your grounds! I have made a free and ingenuous confession of my faith to you. And I could have wished it had been in your hearts to have agreed that some friendly and cordial debates might have been toward mutual conviction. Was there none amongst you to move such a thing? No fitness to listen to it? No desire of a right understanding? If it be not folly in me to listen to town talk, such things have been proposed; and rejected, with stiffness and severity, once and again. Was it not likely to have been more advantageous to the good of this nation? I will say this to you for myself; and to that I have my conscience as a thousand witnesses, and I have my comfort and contentment in it; and I have the witness too of divers here, who I think truly would scorn to own me in a lie: That I would not have been averse to any alteration, of the good of which I might have been convinced. Although I could not have agreed to the taking it off the foundation on which it stands; namely, the acceptance and consent of the people.

I will not presage what you have been about, or doing, in all this time. Nor do I love to make conjectures. But I must tell you this: That as I undertook this government in the simplicity of my heart and as before God, and to do the part of an honest man, and to be true to the interest – which in my conscience 'I think' is dear to many of you; though it is not always understood what God in His wisdom may hide from us, as to peace and settlement:– so I can say that no particular interest, either of myself, estate, honor, or family, are, or have been, prevalent with me to this undertaking. For if you had, upon the old government, offered me this one, this one thing – I speak as thus advised, and before God; as having been to this day of this opinion; and this hath been my constant judgment, well known to many who hear me speak:– if, 'I say', this one thing had been inserted, this one thing, that the government should have been placed in my family hereditary, I would have rejected it. And I could have done no other according to my present conscience and light. I will tell you my reason;– though I cannot tell what God will do with me, nor with you, nor with the nation, for throwing away precious opportunities committed to us.

Now to speak a word or two to you. Of that, I must profess in the name of the same Lord, and wish there had been no cause that I should have thus spoken to you! I told you that I came with joy the first time; with some regret the second; yet now I speak with most regret of all! I look upon you as having among you many persons that I could lay down my life individually for. I could, through the grace of God, desire to lay down my life for you. So far am I from having an unkind or unchristian heart towards you in your particular capacities! I have this indeed as a work most incumbent upon me; this of speaking these things to you. I consulted what might be my duty in such a day as this; casting up all considerations. I must confess, as I told you, that I did think occasionally, this nation had suffered extremely in the respects mentioned; as also in the disappointment of their expectations of that justice which was due to them by your sitting thus long. 'Sitting thus long;' and what have you brought forth? I did not nor cannot comprehend what it is. I would be loath to call it a fate; that were too paganish a word. But there hath been something in it that we had not in our expectations.

I did think also, for myself, that I am like to meet with difficulties; and that this nation will not, as it is fit it should not, be deluded with pretexts of necessity in that great business of raising money. And were it not that I can make some dilemmas upon which to resolve some things of my conscience, judgment and actions, I should shrink at the very prospect of my encounters. Some of them are general, some are more special. Supposing this cause or this business must be carried on, it is either of God or of man. If it be of man, I would I had never touched it with a finger. If I had not had a hope fixed in me that this cause and this business was of God, I would many years ago have run from it. If it be of God, He will bear it up. If it be of man, it will tumble; as everything that hath been of man since the world began hath done. And what are all our histories, and other traditions of actions in former times, but God manifesting Himself, that He hath shaken, and tumbled down and trampled upon, everything that He had not planted? And as this is, so let the All-wise God deal with it. If this be of human structure and invention, and if it be an old plotting and contriving to bring things to this issue, and that they are not the births of Providence – then they will tumble. But if the Lord take pleasure in England, and if He will do us good – He is very able to bear us up! Let the difficulties be whatsoever they will, we shall in His strength be able to encounter with them. And I bless God I have been inured to difficulties; and I never found God failing when I trusted in Him. I can laugh and sing, in my heart, when I speak of these things to you or elsewhere. And though some may think it is a hard thing to raise money without Parliamentary authority upon this nation; yet I have another argument to the good people of this nation, if they would be safe, and yet have no better principle: Whether they prefer the having of their will though it be their destruction, rather than comply with things of necessity? That will excuse me. But I should wrong my native country to suppose this.

For I look at the people of these nations as the blessing of the Lord: and they are a people blessed by God. They have been so; and they will be so, by reason of that immortal seed which hath been, and is, among them: those regenerated ones in the land, of several judgments; who are all the flock of Christ, and lambs of Christ.

We know the Lord hath poured this nation from vessel to vessel till He poured it into your lap, when you came first together. I am confident that it came so into your hands; and was not judged by you to be from counterfeited or feigned necessity, but by Divine providence and dispensation. And this I speak with more earnestness, because I speak for God and not for men. I would have any man to come and tell of the transactions that have been, and of those periods of time wherein God hath made these revolutions; and find where he can fix a feigned necessity! I could recite particulars, if either my strength would serve me to speak, or yours to hear. If you would consider the great hand of God in His great dispensations, you would find that there is scarce a man who fell off, at any period of time when God had any work to do, who can give God or His work at this day a good word.

'It was,' say some, 'the cunning of the Lord Protector' – I take it to myself – 'it was the graft of such a man, and his plot, that hath brought it about!' And, as they say in other countries, 'There are five or six cunning men in England that have skill; they do all these things.' Oh, what blasphemy is this! Because men that are without God in the world, and walk not with Him, know not what it is to pray or believe, and to receive returns from God, and to be spoken unto by the Spirit of God – who speaks without a Written Word sometimes, yet according to it! God hath spoken heretofore in divers manners. Let Him speak as He pleaseth. Hath He not given us liberty, nay, is it not our duty to go to the law and the testimony? And there we shall find that there have been impressions, in extraordinary cases, as well without the Written Word as with it. And therefore there is no difference in the thing thus asserted from truths generally received – except we will exclude the Spirit; without whose concurrence all other teachings are ineffectual. He doth speak to the hearts and consciences of men; and leadeth them to His law and testimony.

There is another necessity, which you have put upon us, and we have not sought. I appeal to God, angels and men – if I shall 'now' raise money according to the article in the government, whether I am not compelled to do it! Which 'government' had power to call you hither; and did;– and instead of seasonably providing for the army, you have labored to overthrow the government, and the army is now upon free-quarter! And you would never so much as let me hear a tittle from you concerning it. Where is the fault? Has it not been as if you had a purpose to put this extremity upon us and the nation? I hope this was not in your minds. I am not willing to judge so:– but such is the state into which we are reduced. By the designs of some in the army who are now in custody it was designed to get as many of them as possible – through discontent for want of money, the army being in a barren country, near thirty weeks behind in pay, and upon other specious pretences – to march for England out of Scotland; and, in discontent, to seize their General there [General Monk], a faithful and honest man, that so another [Colonel Overton] might head the army. And all this opportunity taken from your delays. Whether will this be a thing of feigned necessity? What could it signify, but 'The army are in discontent already; and we will make them live upon stones; we will make them cast off their governors and discipline?' What can be said to this? I list not to unsaddle myself, and put the fault upon your backs. Whether it hath been for the good of England, whilst men have been talking of this thing or the other, and pretending liberty and many good words – whether it has been as it should have been? I am confident you cannot think it has. The nation will not think so. And if the worst should be made of things, I know not what the Cornish men nor the Lincolnshire men may think, or other countries; but I believe they will all think they are not safe. A temporary suspension of 'caring for the greatest liberties and privileges' (if it were so, which is denied) would not have been of such damage as the not providing against free-quarter hath run the nation upon. And if it be my 'liberty' to walk abroad in the fields, or to take a journey, yet it is not my wisdom to do so when my house is on fire!

I have troubled you with a long speech; and I believe it may not have the same resentment with all that it hath with some. But because that is unknown to me, I shall leave it to God;– and conclude with this: That I think myself bound, as in my duty to God, and to the people of these nations for their safety and good in every respect – I think it my duty to tell you that it is not for the profit of these nations, nor for common and public good, for you to continue here any longer. And therefore I do declare unto you, that I do dissolve this Parliament.

PATRICK HENRY (1736–1799)

With very little formal education, Patrick Henry became one of the great orators of the American Revolution. He entered politics at the age of twenty, and went on to become governor of Virginia. In 1775 he delivered this rousing speech before the Virginia Convention of Delegates.

Mr President: No man thinks more highly than I do of the patriotism, as well as abilities, of the very worthy gentlemen who have just addressed the House. But different men often see the same subject in different lights; and, therefore, I hope that it will not be thought disrespectful to those gentlemen, if, entertaining as I do, opinions of a character very opposite to theirs, I shall speak forth my sentiments freely and without reserve. This is no time for ceremony. The question before the House is one of awful moment to this country. For my own part I consider it as nothing less than a question of freedom or slavery; and in proportion to the magnitude of the subject ought to be the freedom of the debate. It is only in this way that we can hope to arrive at truth, and fulfil the great responsibility which we hold to God and our country. Should I keep back my opinions at such a time, through fear of giving offence, I should consider myself as guilty of treason towards my country, and of an act of disloyalty towards the majesty of heaven, which I revere above all earthly kings.

Mr President, it is natural to man to indulge in the illusions of hope. We are apt to shut our eyes against a painful truth, and listen to the song of that siren, till she transforms us into beasts. Is this the part of wise men, engaged in a great and arduous struggle for liberty? Are we disposed to be of the number of those who, having eyes, see not, and having ears, hear not, the things which so nearly concern their temporal salvation? For my part, whatever anguish of spirit it may cost, I am willing to know the whole truth; to know the worst and to provide for it.

I have but one lamp by which my feet are guided; and that is the lamp of experience. I know of no way of judging of the future but by the past. And judging by the past, I wish to know what there has been in the conduct of the British ministry for the last ten years, to justify those hopes with which gentlemen have been pleased to solace themselves and the House? Is it that insidious smile with which our petition has been lately received? Trust it not, sir; it will prove a snare to your feet. Suffer not yourselves to be betrayed with a kiss. Ask yourselves how this gracious reception of our petition comports with these war-like preparations which cover our waters and darken our land. Are fleets and armies necessary to a work of love and reconciliation? Have we shown ourselves so unwilling to be reconciled, that force must be called in to win back our love? Let us not deceive ourselves, sir. These are implements of war and subjugation; the last arguments to which kings resort. I ask gentlemen, sir, what means this martial array, if its purpose be not to force us to submission? Can gentlemen assign any other possible motives for it? Has Great Britain any enemy, in this quarter of the world, to call for all this accumulation of navies and armies? No, sir, she has none. They are meant for us; they can be meant for no other. They are sent over to bind and rivet upon us those chains which the British ministry have been so long forging.

And what have we to oppose to them? Shall we try argument? Sir, we have been trying that for the last ten years. Have we anything new to offer on the subject? Nothing. We have held the subject up in every light of which it is capable; but it has been all in vain. Shall we resort to entreaty and humble supplication? What terms shall we find which have not been already exhausted? Let us not, I beseech you, sir, deceive ourselves longer. Sir, we have done everything that could be done, to avert the storm which is now coming on. We have petitioned; we have remonstrated; we have supplicated; we have prostrated ourselves before the throne, and have implored its interposition to arrest the tyrannical hands of the ministry and Parliament. Our petitions have been slighted; our remonstrances have produced additional violence and insult; our supplications have been disregarded; and we have been spurned, with contempt, from the foot of the throne. In vain, after these things, may we indulge the fond hope of peace and reconciliation. There is no longer any room for hope. If we wish to be free – if we mean to preserve inviolate those inestimable privileges for which we have been so long contending – if we mean not basely to abandon the noble struggle in which we have been so long engaged, and which we have pledged ourselves never to abandon until the glorious object of our contest shall be obtained, we must fight! I repeat it, sir, we must fight! An appeal to arms and to the God of Hosts is all that is left us!

They tell us, sir, that we are weak; unable to cope with so formidable an adversary. But when shall we be stronger? Will it be the next week, or the next year? Will it be when we are totally disarmed, and when a British guard shall be stationed in every house? Shall we gather strength by irresolution and inaction? Shell we acquire the means of effectual resistance, by lying supinely on our backs, and hugging the delusive phantom of hope, until our enemies shall have bound us hand and foot? Sir, we are not weak, if we make a proper use of the means which the God of nature hath placed in our power. Three millions of people, armed in the holy cause of liberty, and in such a country as that which we possess, are invincible by any force which our enemy can send against us. Besides, sir, we shall not fight our battles alone. There is a just God who presides over the destinies of nations; and who will raise up friends to fight our battles for us. The battle, sir, is not to the strong alone; it is to the vigilant, the active, the brave. Besides, sir, we have no election. If we were base enough to desire it, it is now too late to retire from the contest. There is no retreat, but in submission and slavery! Our chains are forged! Their clanking may be heard on the plains of Boston! The war is inevitable – and let it come! I repeat it, sir, let it come!

It is in vain, sir, to extenuate the matter. Gentlemen may cry peace, peace – but there is no peace. The war is actually begun! The next gale that sweeps from the north will bring to our ears the clash of resounding arms! Our brethren are already in the field! Why stand we here idle? What is it that gentlemen wish? What would they have? Is life so dear, or peace so sweet, as to be purchased at the price of chains and slavery? Forbid it, Almighty God! I know not what course others may take; but as for me, give me liberty, or give me death!

NEVILLE CHAMBERLAIN (1869–1940)

British prime minister from 1937 to 1940, Chamberlain is remembered for his ambitious attempt to secure peace between Britain and Germany through the signing of the Munich Pact, as well as for this now notorious 1938 speech declaring 'peace for our time' just months before the outbreak of the Second World War.

My good friends, this is the second time in our history that there has come back from Germany to Downing Street peace with honour. (Cheering.) I believe it is peace for our time. We thank you from the bottom of our hearts. (To this the crowd responded: 'We thank you. God bless you.') And now I recommend you to go home and sleep quietly in your beds.

WINSTON CHURCHILL (1874–1965)

A soldier and eloquent orator, Winston Churchill succeeded
Neville Chamberlain — whose policy of appeasement he
vehemently disagreed with — as Prime Minister of Great
Britain in 1940. A month after his appointment, before
the House of Commons, he told his epic story of the defense
of Dunkirk.

From the moment when the defenses at Sedan on the
Meuse were broken at the end of the second week in May
only a rapid retreat to Amiens and the south could have
saved the British–French armies who had entered Belgium
at the appeal of the Belgian King.

This strategic fact was not immediately realized.
The French High Command hoped it would be able to
close the gap. The armies of the north were under their
orders. Moreover, a retirement of that kind would have
involved almost certainly the destruction of a fine Belgian
Army of twenty divisions and abandonment of the Whole
of Belgium.

Therefore, when the force and scope of the German
penetration was realized and when the new French
Generalissimo, General [Maxime] Weygand, assumed command in place of General Gamelin, an effort was made by
the French and British Armies in Belgium to keep holding
the right hand of the Belgians and give their own right hand
to the newly created French Army which was to advance
across the Somme in great strength.

However, the German eruption swept like a sharp
scythe south of Amiens to the rear of the armies in the

north – eight or nine armored divisions, each with about 400 armored vehicles of different kinds divisible into small self-contained units.

This force cut off all communications between us and the main French Army. It severed our communications for food and ammunition. It ran first through Amiens, afterwards through Abbeville, and it shore its way up the coast to Boulogne and Calais, almost to Dunkirk.

Behind this armored and mechanized onslaught came a number of German divisions in lorries, and behind them, again, plodded comparatively slowly the dull, brute mass of the ordinary German Army and German people, always ready to be led to the trampling down in other lands of liberties and comforts they never have known in their own.

I said this armored scythe stroke almost reached Dunkirk – almost but not quite. Boulogne and Calais were scenes of desperate fighting. The guards defended Boulogne for a while and were then withdrawn by orders from this country.

The rifle brigade of the Sixtieth Rifles (Queen Victoria's Rifles), with a battalion of British tanks and 1,000 Frenchmen, in all about 4,000 strong, defended Calais to the last. The British brigadier was given an hour to surrender. He spurned the offer. Four days of intense street fighting passed before the silence reigned in Calais which marked the end of a memorable resistance.

Only thirty unwounded survivors were brought off by the navy, and we do not know the fate of their comrades. Their sacrifice was not, however, in vain. At least two armored divisions which otherwise would have been turned against the BEF had to be sent to overcome them. They have added another page to the glories of the light division.

The time gained enabled the Gravelines water line to be flooded and held by French troops. Thus the port of Dunkirk was held open. When it was found impossible for the armies of the north to reopen their communications through Amiens with the main French armies, only one choice remained. It seemed, indeed, a forlorn hope. The Belgian and French armies were almost surrounded. Their sole line of retreat was to a single port and its neighboring beaches. They were pressed on every side by heavy attacks and were far outnumbered in the air.

When a week ago today I asked the House to fix this afternoon for the occasion of a statement, I feared it would be my hard lot to announce from this box the greatest military disaster of our long history.

I thought, and there were good judges who agreed with me, that perhaps 20,000 or 30,000 men might be re-embarked, but it certainly seemed that the whole French First Army and the whole BEF, north of the Amiens–Abbeville gap would be broken up in open field or else have to capitulate for lack of food and ammunition.

These were the hard and heavy tidings I called on the House and nation to prepare themselves for.

The whole root and core and brain of the British Army, around which and upon which we were building and are able to build the great British armies of later years, seemed due to perish upon the field. That was the prospect a week ago, but another blow which might have proved final was still to fall upon us.

The King of the Belgians called upon us to come to his aid. Had not this ruler and his government severed themselves from the Allies who rescued their country from extinction in the late war, and had they not sought refuge in what has been proved to be fatal neutrality, then the French and British armies at the outset might well have saved not only Belgium but perhaps even Holland.

At the last moment, when Belgium was already invaded, King Leopold called upon us to come to his aid, and even at the last moment we came. He and his brave and efficient army of nearly half a million strong guarded our eastern flank; this kept open our only retreat to the sea.

Suddenly, without any prior consultation and with the least possible notice, without the advice of his ministers and on his own personal act, he sent a plenipotentiary to the German Command surrendering his army and exposing our flank and the means of retreat.

I asked the House a week ago to suspend its judgment because the facts were not clear. I do not think there is now any reason why we should not form our own opinions upon this pitiful episode. The surrender of the Belgian Army compelled the British Army at the shortest notice to cover a flank to the sea of more than thirty miles' length which otherwise would have been cut off.

In doing this and closing this flank, contact was lost inevitably between the British and two of three corps forming the First French Army who were then further from the coast than we were. It seemed impossible that large numbers of Allied troops could reach the coast. The enemy attacked on all sides in great strength and fierceness, and their main power, air force, was thrown into the battle.

The enemy began to fire cannon along the beaches by which alone shipping could approach or depart. They sowed magnetic mines in the channels and seas and sent repeated waves of hostile aircraft, sometimes more than 100 strong, to cast bombs on a single pier that remained and on the sand dunes.

Their U-boats, one of which was sunk, and motor launches took their toll of the vast traffic which now began. For four or five days the intense struggle raged. All armored divisions, or what was left of them, together with great masses of German infantry and artillery, hurled themselves on the ever narrowing and contracting appendix within which the British and French armies fought.

Meanwhile the Royal Navy, with the willing help of countless merchant seamen and a host of volunteers, strained every nerve and every effort and every craft to embark the British and Allied troops.

Over 220 light warships and more than 650 other vessels were engaged. They had to approach this difficult coast, often in adverse weather, under an almost ceaseless hail of bombs and increasing concentration of artillery fire. Nor were the seas themselves free from mines and torpedoes.

It was in conditions such as these that our men carried on with little or no rest for days and nights, moving troops across dangerous waters and bringing with them always the men whom they had rescued. The numbers they brought back are the measure of their devotion and their courage.

Hospital ships, which were plainly marked, were the special target for Nazi bombs, but the men and women aboard them never faltered in their duty.

Meanwhile the RAF, who already had been intervening in the battle so far as its range would allow it to go from home bases, now used a part of its main metropolitan fighter strength to strike at German bombers.

The struggle was protracted and fierce. Suddenly the scene has cleared. The crash and thunder has momentarily, but only for the moment, died away. The miracle of deliverance achieved by the valor and perseverance, perfect discipline, faultless service, skill and unconquerable vitality is a manifesto to us all.

The enemy was hurled back by the British and French troops. He was so roughly handled that he dare not molest their departure seriously. The air force decisively defeated the main strength of the German Air Force and inflicted on them a loss of at least four to one.

The navy, using nearly 1,000 ships of all kinds, carried over 335,000 men, French and British, from the jaws of death back to their native land and to the tasks which lie immediately before them.

We must be very careful not to assign to this deliverance attributes of a victory. Wars are not won by evacuations, but there was a victory inside this deliverance which must be noted.

Many of our soldiers coming back have not seen the air force at work. They only saw the bombers which escaped their protective attack. This was a great trial of strength between the British and German Air Forces.

Can you conceive of a greater objective for the power of Germany in the air than to make all evacuations from these beaches impossible and to sink all of the ships, numbering almost 1,000? Could there have been an incentive of greater military importance and significance to the whole purpose of the war?

They tried hard and were beaten back. They were frustrated in their task; we have got the armies away and they have paid fourfold for any losses sustained. Very large formations of German airplanes were turned on several occasions from the attack by a quarter their number of RAF planes and dispersed in different directions. Twelve airplanes have been hunted by two. One airplane was driven into the water and cast away by the charge of a British airplane which had no more ammunition.

All of our types and our pilots have been vindicated. The Hurricane, Spitfires and Defiance have been vindicated. When I consider how much greater would be our advantage in defending the air above this island against overseas attacks, I find in these facts a sure basis on which practical and reassuring thoughts may rest, and I will pay my tribute to these young airmen.

May it not be that the cause of civilization itself will be defended by the skill and devotion of a few thousand airmen? There never has been, I suppose, in all the history of the world such opportunity for youth.

The Knights of the Round Table and the Crusaders have fallen back into distant days, not only distant but prosaic; but these young men are going forth every morning, going forth holding in their hands an instrument of colossal shattering power, of whom it may be said that every morn brought forth a noble chance and every chance brought forth a noble deed. These young men deserve our gratitude, as all brave men who in so many ways and so many occasions are ready and will continue to be ready to give their life and their all to their native land.

I return to the army. In a long series of very fierce battles, now on this front, now on that, fighting on three fronts at once, battles fought by two or three divisions against an equal or sometimes larger number of the enemy, and fought very fiercely on old ground so many of us knew so well, our losses in men exceed 30,000 in killed, wounded and missing. I take this occasion for expressing the sympathy of the House with those who have suffered bereavement or are still anxious.

The President of the Board of Trade (Sir Andrew Duncan) is not here today. His son has been killed, and many here have felt private affliction of the sharpest form, but I would say about the missing – we have had a large number of wounded come home safely to this country – there may be very many reported missing who will come back home some day.

In the confusion of departure it is inevitable that many should be cut off. Against this loss of over 30,000 men we may set the far heavier loss certainly inflicted on the enemy, but our losses in material are enormous. We have perhaps lost one-third of the men we lost in the opening days of the battle on March 21, 1918, but we have lost nearly as many guns – nearly 1,000 – and all our transport and all the armored vehicles that were with the army of the north.

These losses will impose further delay on the expansion of our military strength. That expansion has not been proceeding as fast as we had hoped. The best of all we had to give has been given to the BEF, and although they had not the number of tanks and some articles of equipment which were desirable they were a very well and finely equipped army. They had the first fruits of all our industry had to give. That has gone and now here is further delay.

How long it will be, how long it will last depends upon the exertions which we make on this island. An effort, the like of which has never been seen in our records, is now being made. Work is proceeding night and day, Sundays and week days. Capital and labor have cast aside their interests, rights and customs and put everything into the common stock. Already the flow of munitions has leaped forward. There is no reason why we should not in a few months overtake the sudden and serious loss that has come upon us without retarding the development of our general program.

Nevertheless, our thankfulness at the escape of our army with so many men, and the thankfulness of their loved ones, who passed through an agonizing week, must not blind us to the fact that what happened in France and Belgium is a colossal military disaster.

The French Army has been weakened, the Belgian Army has been lost and a large part of those fortified lines upon which so much faith was reposed has gone, and many valuable mining districts and factories have passed into the enemy's possession.

The whole of the channel ports are in his hands, with all the strategic consequences that follow from that, and we must expect another blow to be struck almost immediately at us or at France.

We were told that Hitler has plans for invading the British Isles. This has often been thought of before. When Napoleon lay at Boulogne for a year with his flat-bottomed boats and his Grand Army, someone told him there were bitter weeds in England. There certainly were and a good many more of them have since been returned. The whole question of defense against invasion is powerfully affected by the fact that we have for the time being in this island incomparably more military forces than we had in the last war. But this will not continue. We shall not be content with a defensive war. We have our duty to our Allies.

We have to reconstitute and build up the BEF once again under its gallant Commander in Chief, Lord Gort. All this is en train. But now I feel we must put our defense in this island into such a high state of organization that the fewest possible numbers will be required to give effectual security and that the largest possible potential offensive effort may be released.

On this we are now engaged. It would be very convenient to enter upon this subject in secret sessions. The government would not necessarily be able to reveal any great military secrets, but we should like to have our discussions free and without the restraint imposed by the fact that they would be read the next day by the enemy.

The government would benefit by the views expressed by the House. I understand that some request is to be made on this subject, which will be readily acceded to by the government. We have found it necessary to take measures of increasing stringency, not only against enemy aliens and suspicious characters of other nationalities but also against British subjects who may become a danger or a nuisance should the war be transported to the United Kingdom.

I know there are a great many people affected by the orders which we have made who are passionate enemies of

Nazi Germany. I am very sorry for them, but we cannot, under the present circumstances, draw all the distinctions we should like to do. If parachute landings were attempted and fierce fights followed, those unfortunate people would be far better out of the way for their own sake as well as ours.

There is, however, another class for which I feel not the slightest sympathy. Parliament has given us powers to put down fifth column activities with the strongest hand, and we shall use those powers subject to the supervision and correction of the House without hesitation until we are satisfied and more than satisfied that this malignancy in our midst has been effectually stamped out.

Turning once again to the question of invasion, there has, I will observe, never been a period in all those long centuries of which we boast when an absolute guarantee against invasion, still less against serious raids, could have been given to our people. In the days of Napoleon the same wind which might have carried his transports across the Channel might have driven away a blockading fleet. There is always the chance, and it is that chance which has excited and befooled the imaginations of many continental tyrants.

We are assured that novel methods will be adopted, and when we see the originality, malice and ingenuity of aggression which our enemy displays we may certainly prepare ourselves for every kind of novel stratagem and every kind of brutal and treacherous manoeuvre. I think no idea is so outlandish that it should not be considered and viewed with a watchful, but at the same time steady, eye.

We must never forget the solid assurances of sea power and those which belong to air power if they can be locally exercised. I have myself full confidence that if all do their duty and if the best arrangements are made, as they are being made, we shall prove ourselves once again able to defend our island home, ride out the storms of war and outlive the menace of tyranny, if necessary, for years, if necessary, alone.

At any rate, that is what we are going to try to do. That is the resolve of His Majesty's Government, every man of them. That is the will of Parliament and the nation. The British Empire and the French Republic, linked together in their cause and their need, will defend to the death their native soils, aiding each other like good comrades to the utmost of their strength, even though a large tract of Europe and many old and famous States have fallen or may fall into the grip of the Gestapo and all the odious apparatus of Nazi rule.

We shall not flag nor fail. We shall go on to the end. We shall fight in France and on the seas and oceans; we shall fight with growing confidence and growing strength in the air.

We shall defend our island whatever the cost may be; we shall fight on beaches, landing grounds, in fields, in streets and on the hills. We shall never surrender and even if, which I do not for the moment believe, this island or a large part of it were subjugated and starving, then our empire beyond the seas, armed and guarded by the British Fleet, will carry on the struggle until in God's good time the New World, with all its power and might, sets forth to the liberation and rescue of the Old.

ALBERT EINSTEIN (1879–1955)

In 1939 Albert Einstein sent a letter to President Roosevelt, explaining the possibility of using atomic energy to create weapons — this sparked the beginning of atomic research by the government. The following speech calls for peace between nations, and was televised in 1950, five years after the bombing of Hiroshima.

I am grateful to you for the opportunity to express my conviction in this most important political question.

The idea of achieving security through national armament is, at the present state of military technique, a disastrous illusion. On the part of the United States this illusion had been particularly fostered by the fact that this country succeeded first in producing an atomic bomb. The belief seemed to prevail that in the end it were possible to achieve decisive military superiority.

In this way, any potential opponent would be intimidated, and security, so ardently desired by all of us, brought to us and all of humanity. The maxim which we have been following during these last five years has been, in short: security through superior military power, whatever the cost.

The armament race between the USA and the USSR, originally supposed to be a preventive measure, assumes hysterical character. On both sides, the means to mass destruction are perfected with feverish haste – behind the respective walls of secrecy. The H-bomb appears on the public horizon as a probably attainable goal.

If successful, radioactive poisoning of the atmosphere and hence annihilation of any life on earth has been brought within the range of technical possibilities. The ghostlike character of this development lies in its apparently compulsory trend. Every step appears as the unavoidable consequence of the preceding one. In the end, there beckons more and more clearly general annihilation.

Is there any way out of this impasse created by man himself? All of us, and particularly those who are responsible for the attitude of the US and the USSR, should realize that we may have vanquished an external enemy, but have been incapable of getting rid of the mentality created by the war.

It is impossible to achieve peace as long as every single action is taken with a possible future conflict in view. The leading point of view of all political action should therefore be: What can we do to bring about a peaceful co-existence and even loyal cooperation of the nations?

The first problem is to do away with mutual fear and distrust. Solemn renunciation of violence (not only with respect to means of mass destruction) is undoubtedly necessary.

Such renunciation, however, can only be effective if at the same time a supra-national judicial and executive body is set up empowered to decide questions of immediate concern to the security of the nations. Even a declaration of the nations to collaborate loyally in the realization of such a 'restricted world government' would considerably reduce the imminent danger of war.

In the last analysis, every kind of peaceful cooperation among men is primarily based on mutual trust and only secondly on institutions such as courts of justice and police. This holds for nations as well as for individuals. And the basis of trust is loyal give and take.

POLITICAL

SPEECHES

NIKOLAI LENIN (1870–1924)

Theoretician and revolutionary, Nikolai Lenin was leader of the communist Bolshevik party. In 1917, when the Bolsheviks overthrew Premier Aleksandr Kerensky's weak provisional government and established a Soviet government, Lenin became Russia's first dictator. He made this speech in defense of proletarian dictatorship in 1919.

The growth of the revolutionary movement of the proletariat in all countries has called forth convulsive efforts of the bourgeoisie and its agents in workmen's organizations, to find ideal political arguments in defense of the rule of the exploiters. Among these arguments stands out particularly condemnation of dictatorship and defense of democracy. The falseness and hypocrisy of such an argument, which has been repeated in thousands of forms in the capitalist press and at the conference of the yellow International in February, 1919, Berne, are evident to all who have not wished to betray the fundamental principle of socialism.

First of all, this argument is used with certain interpretations of 'democracy in general' and 'dictatorship in general' without raising the point as to which class one has in mind. Such a statement of the question, leaving out of consideration the question of class as though it were a general national matter, is direct mockery of the fundamental doctrine of socialism, namely, the doctrine of class struggle, which the socialists who have gone over to the side of the bourgeoisie recognize when they talk, but forget when they act. For in no civilized capitalist country does there exist 'democracy in general,' but there exists only bourgeois democracy, and one is speaking not of 'dictatorship in general' but of dictatorship of the oppressed classes, that is, of the proletariat with respect to the oppressors and exploiters, that is, the bourgeoisie, in order to overcome the resistance which the exploiters make in their struggle to preserve their rule.

History teaches that no oppressed class has ever come into power and cannot come into power, without passing through a period of dictatorship, that is, the conquest of power and the forcible suppression of the most desperate and mad resistance which does not hesitate to resort to any crimes, such has always been shown by the exploiters. The bourgeoisie, whose rule is now defended by the socialists who speak against 'dictatorship in general' and who espouse the cause of 'democracy in general', has won power in the progressive countries at the price of a series of uprisings, civil wars, forcible suppression of kinds, feudal lords, and slave owners, and of their attempts at restoration. The socialists of all countries in their books and pamphlets, in the resolutions of their congresses, in their propaganda speeches, have explained to the people thousands and millions of times the class character of these bourgeois revolutions, and of this bourgeois dictatorship. Therefore the present defense of bourgeois democracy in the form of speeches about 'democracy in general', and the present wails and shouts against the dictatorship of the proletariat in the form of wails about 'dictatorship in general', are a direct mockery of socialism, and represent in fact going over to the bourgeoisie and denying the right of the proletariat to its own proletariat revolution, and a defense of bourgeois reformism, precisely at the historic moment when bourgeois reformism is collapsing the world over, and when the war has created a revolutionary situation.

All socialists who explain the class character of bourgeois civilisation, or bourgeois democracy, of bourgeois parliamentarism, express the thought which Marx and Engels expressed with the most scientific exactness when they said that the most democratic bourgeois republic is nothing more than a machine for the suppression of the working class by the bourgeoisie, for the suppression of the mass of the toilers by a handful of capitalists. There is not a single revolutionist, not a single Marxist of all those who are now shouting against dictatorship and for democracy, who would not have sworn before the workmen that he recognizes this fundamental truth of socialism. And now, when the revolutionary proletariat begins to act and move for the destruction of this machinery of oppression, and to win the proletarian dictatorship, these traitors to socialism report the situation as though the bourgeoisie were giving the laborers pure democracy, as though the bourgeoisie were abandoning resistance and were ready to submit to the majority of the toilers, as though there were no state machinery for the suppression of labor by capital in a democratic republic.

Workmen know very well that 'freedom of meetings', even in the most democratic bourgeois republic is an empty phrase, for the rich have all the best public and private buildings at their disposal, and also sufficient leisure time for meetings and for protection of these meetings by the bourgeois apparatus of authority. The proletarians of the city and of the village, and the poor peasants, that is, the overwhelming majority of the population, have none of these three things. So long as the situation is such, 'equality', that is, 'pure democracy', is sheer fraud.

The capitalists have always called 'freedom' the freedom to make money for the rich, and the freedom to die of hunger for workmen. The capitalists call 'freedom' the freedom of the rich, freedom to buy up the press, to use wealth, to manufacture and support so-called public opinion. The defenders of 'pure democracy' again in actual fact turn out to be the defenders of the most dirty and corrupt system of the rule of the rich over the means of education of the masses. They deceive the people by attractive, fine-sounding, beautiful but absolutely false phrases, trying to dissuade the masses from the concrete historic task of freeing the press from the capitalists who have gotten control of it. Actual freedom and equality will exist only in the order established by the Communist, in which it will be impossible to become rich at the expense of another, where it will be impossible either directly or indirectly to subject the press to power of money, where there will be no obstacle to prevent any toiler from enjoying and actually realizing the equal right to the use of public printing presses and of the public fund of paper.

Dictatorship of the proletariat resembles dictatorship of other classes in that it was called forth by the need to suppress the forcible resistance of a class that was losing its political rulership. But that which definitely distinguishes a dictatorship of the proletariat from a dictatorship of other classes, from a dictatorship of the bourgeoisie in all the civilized capitalist countries, is that the dictatorship of the landlords and of the bourgeoisie was the forcible suppression of the resistance of the overwhelming majority of the population, namely, the toilers. On the other hand, the dictatorship of the proletariat is the forcible suppression of the resistance of the exploiters, that is, of an insignificant minority of the population – of landlords and capitalists.

It therefore follows that a dictatorship of the proletariat must necessarily carry with it not only changes in the form and institutions of democracy, speaking in general terms, but specifically such a change as would secure an extension such as has never been seen in the history of the world of the actual use of democratism by the toiling classes.

FRANKLIN D. ROOSEVELT (1882–1945)

The only American President to serve three consecutive terms,
Franklin D. Roosevelt led the US through difficult years
from 1933 to 1945. Remembered as a charismatic, dashing,
optimistic leader, Roosevelt delivered this uplifting inaugural
address to a nation demoralised by the worst depression
America had ever known.

This is a day of national consecration.

I am certain that my fellow Americans expect that on
my induction into the presidency I will address them with
a candor and a decision which the present situation of
our nation impels. This is preeminently the time to speak
the truth, the whole truth, frankly and boldly. Nor need
we shrink from honestly facing conditions in our country today. This great nation will endure as it has endured,
will revive and will prosper. So, first of all, let me assert
my firm belief that the only thing we have to fear is fear
itself – nameless, unreasoning, unjustified terror which
paralyzes needed efforts to convert retreat into advance. In
every dark hour of our national life a leadership of frank-
ness and vigor has met with that understanding and support
of the people themselves which is essential to victory. I am
convinced that you will again give that support to leadership in these critical days.

In such a spirit on my part and on yours we face our
common difficulties. They concern, thank God, only material things. Values have shrunken to fantastic levels; taxes
have risen; our ability to pay has fallen; government of
all kinds is faced by serious curtailment of income; the

means of exchange are frozen in the currents of trade; the withered leaves of industrial enterprise lie on every side; farmers find no markets for their produce; the savings of many years in thousands of families are gone.

More important, a host of unemployed citizens face the grim problem of existence, and an equally great number toil with little return. Only a foolish optimist can deny the dark realities of the moment.

Yet our distress comes from no failure of substance. We are stricken by no plague of locusts. Compared with the perils which our forefathers conquered because they believed and were not afraid, we have still much to be thankful for. Nature still offers her bounty, and human efforts have multiplied it. Plenty is at our doorstep, but a generous use of it languishes in the very sight of the supply. Primarily this is because rulers of the exchange of mankind's goods have failed through their own stubbornness and their own incompetence, have admitted their failure, and have abdicated. Practices of the unscrupulous money changers stand indicted in the court of public opinion, rejected by the hearts and minds of men.

True, they have tried, but their efforts have been cast in the pattern of an outworn tradition. Faced by failure of credit, they have proposed only the lending of more money. Stripped of the lure of profit by which to induce our people to follow their false leadership, they have resorted to exhortations, pleading tearfully for restored confidence. They know only the rules of a generation of self-seekers. They have no vision, and when there is no vision the people perish.

The money changers have fled from their high seats in

the temple of our civilization. We may now restore that temple to the ancient truths. The measure of the restoration lies in the extent to which we apply social values more noble than mere monetary profit.

Happiness lies not in the mere possession of money; it lies in the joy of achievement, in the thrill of creative effort. The joy and moral stimulation of work no longer must be forgotten in the mad chase of evanescent profits. These dark days will be worth all they cost us if they teach us that our true destiny is not to be ministered unto but to minister to ourselves and to our fellowmen.

Recognition of the falsity of material wealth as the standard of success goes hand in hand with the abandonment of the false belief that public office and high political position are to be valued only by the standards of pride of place and personal profit; and there must be an end to a conduct in banking and in business which too often has given to a sacred trust the likeness of callous and selfish wrongdoing. Small wonder that confidence languishes, for it thrives only on honesty, on honor, on the sacredness of obligations, on faithful protection, on unselfish performance; without them it cannot live.

Restoration calls, however, not for changes in ethics alone. This nation asks for action, and action now.

Our greatest primary task is to put people to work. This is no unsolvable problem if we face it wisely and courageously. It can be accomplished in part by direct recruiting by the government itself, treating the task as we would treat the emergency of a war, but at the same time, through this employment, accomplishing greatly needed projects to stimulate and reorganize the use of our natural resources.

Hand in hand with this we must frankly recognize the overbalance of population in our industrial centers and, by engaging on a national scale in a redistribution, endeavor to provide a better use of the land for those best fitted for the land. The task can be helped by definite efforts to raise the values of agricultural products and with this the power to purchase the output of our cities. It can be helped by preventing realistically the tragedy of the growing loss through foreclosure of our small homes and our farms. It can be helped by insistence that the federal, state, and local governments act forthwith on the demand that their cost be drastically reduced. It can be helped by the unifying of relief activities, which today are often scattered, uneconomical, and unequal. It can be helped by national planning for and supervision of all forms of transportation and of communications and other utilities which have a definitely public character. There are many ways in which it can be helped, but it can never be helped merely by talking about it. We must act and act quickly.

Finally, in our progress toward a resumption of work we require two safeguards against a return of the evils of the old order: there must be a strict supervision of all banking and credits and investments, so that there will be an end to speculation with other people's money; and there must be provision for an adequate but sound currency.

These are the lines of attack. I shall presently urge upon a new Congress, in special session, detailed measures for their fulfillment, and I shall seek the immediate assistance of the several states.

Through this program of action we address ourselves to putting our own national house in order and making income balance outgo. Our international trade relations, though vastly important, are in point of time and necessity secondary to the establishment of a sound national economy. I favor as a practical policy the putting of first things first. I shall spare no effort to restore world trade by international economic readjustment, but the emergency at home cannot wait on that accomplishment.

The basic thought that guides these specific means of national recovery is not narrowly nationalistic. It is the insistence, as a first consideration, upon the interdependence of the various elements in and parts of the United States – a recognition of the old and permanently important manifestation of the American spirit of the pioneer. It is the way to recovery. It is the immediate way. It is the strongest assurance that the recovery will endure.

In the field of world policy I would dedicate this nation to the policy of the good neighbor – the neighbor who resolutely respects himself and, because he does so, respects the rights of others – the neighbor who respects his obligations and respects the sanctity of his agreements in and with a world of neighbors.

If I read the temper of our people correctly, we now realize as we have never realized before our interdependence on each other; that we cannot merely take but we must give as well; that if we are to go forward, we must move as a trained and loyal army willing to sacrifice for the good of a common discipline, because without such discipline no progress is made, no leadership becomes effective. We are, I know, ready and willing to submit our lives and property to such discipline, because it makes possible a leadership which aims at a larger good. This I propose to offer, pledging that the larger purposes will bind upon us all as a sacred obligation with a unity of duty hitherto evoked only in time of armed strife.

With this pledge taken, I assume unhesitatingly the leadership of this great army of our people dedicated to a disciplined attack upon our common problems.

Action in this image and to this end is feasible under the form of government which we have inherited from our ancestors. Our Constitution is so simple and practical that it is possible always to meet extraordinary needs by changes in emphasis and arrangement without loss of essential form. That is why our constitutional system has proved itself the most superbly enduring political mechanism the modern world has produced. It has met every stress of vast expansion of territory, of foreign wars, of bitter internal strife, of world relations.

It is to be hoped that the normal balance of executive and legislative authority may be wholly adequate to meet the unprecedented task before us. But it may be that an unprecedented demand and need for undelayed action may call for temporary departure from that normal balance of public procedure.

I am prepared under my constitutional duty to recommend the measures that a stricken nation in the midst of a stricken world may require. These measures, or such other measures as the Congress may build out of its experience and wisdom, I shall seek, within my constitutional authority, to bring to speedy adoption.

But in the event that the Congress shall fail to take one of these two courses, and in the event that the national emergency is still critical. I shall not evade the clear course of duty that will then confront me. I shall ask the Congress for the one remaining instrument to meet the crisis – broad executive power to wage a war against the emergency, as great as the power that would be given to me if we were in fact invaded by a foreign foe.

For the trust reposed in me I will return the courage and devotion that befit the time. I can do no less.

We face the arduous days that lie before us in the warm courage of national unity; with the clear consciousness of seeking old and precious moral values; with the clean satisfaction that comes from the stern performance of duty by old and young alike. We aim at the assurance of a rounded and permanent national life.

We do not distrust the future of essential democracy. The people of the United States have not failed. In their need they have registered a mandate that they want direct, vigorous action. They have asked for discipline and direction under leadership. They have made me the present instrument of their wishes. In the spirit of the gift I take it.

In this dedication of a nation we humbly ask the blessing of God. May he protect each and every one of us. May he guide me in the days to come.

JOHN F. KENNEDY (1917–1963)

*In 1961, at the age of forty-three, John F. Kennedy became
the youngest American President in history. Looking back,
Kennedy has been praised for his dedication to improving
civil rights, and for the part he played in avoiding nuclear
war during the Cuban missile crisis. In this, his inaugural
speech, he espoused his commitment to democracy and liberty,
and called for international peace and arms control.*

We observe today not a victory of a party but a celebration
of freedom – symbolizing an end as well as a beginning –
signifying renewal as well as change. For I have sworn
before you and Almighty God the same solemn oath our forebears prescribed nearly a century and three quarters ago.

The world is very different now. For man holds in his
mortal hands the power to abolish all forms of human
poverty and all forms of human life. And yet the same revolutionary beliefs for which our forebears fought are still at
issue around the globe – the belief that the rights of man
come not from the generosity of the state but from the
hand of God.

We dare not forget today that we are the heirs of that
first revolution. Let the word go forth from this time and
place, to friend and foe alike, that the torch has been passed
to a new generation of Americans – born in this century,
tempered by war, disciplined by a hard and bitter peace,
proud of our ancient heritage – and unwilling to witness or
permit slow undoing of those human rights to which this
nation has always been committed, and to which we are
committed today at home and around the world.

Let every nation know, whether it wishes us well or ill, that we shall pay any price, bear any burden, meet any hardship, support any friend, oppose any foe to assure the survival and success of liberty.

This much we pledge – and more. To those old allies whose cultural and spiritual origins we share, we pledge the loyalty of faithful friends. United, there is little we cannot do in a host of cooperative ventures. Divided, there is little we can do – for we dare not meet a powerful challenge at odds and split asunder.

To those new states whom we welcome to the ranks of the free, we pledge our word that one form of colonial control shall not have passed away merely to be replaced by a far more iron tyranny. We shall not always expect to find them supporting our view. But we shall always hope to find them strongly supporting their own freedom – and to remember that, in the past, those who foolishly sought power by riding the back of the tiger ended up inside.

To those peoples in the huts and villages of half the globe struggling to break the bonds of mass misery, we pledge our best efforts to help them help themselves, for whatever period is required – not because the Communists may be doing it, not because we seek their votes, but because it is right. If a free society cannot help the many who are poor, it cannot save the few who are rich.

To our sister republics south of our border, we offer a special pledge – to convert our good words into good deeds – in a new alliance for progress – to assist free men and free governments in casting off the chains of poverty. But this peaceful revolution of hope cannot become the prey of hostile powers. Let all our neighbors know that we shall join with them to oppose aggression or subversion anywhere in the Americas. And let every other power know that this hemisphere intends to remain the master of its own house.

To that world assembly of sovereign states, the United Nations, our last best hope in an age where the instruments of war have far out-paced the instruments of peace, we renew our pledge of support – to prevent it from becoming merely a forum for invective – to strengthen its shield of the new and the weak – and to enlarge the area in which its writ may run.

Finally, to those nations who would make themselves our adversary, we offer not a pledge but a request: that both sides begin anew the quest for peace, before the dark powers of destruction unleashed by science engulf all humanity in planned or accidental self-destruction.

We dare not tempt them with weakness. For only when our arms are sufficient beyond doubt can we be certain beyond doubt that they will never be employed.

But neither can two great and powerful groups of nations take comfort from our present course – both sides overburdened by the cost of modern weapons, both rightly alarmed by the steady spread of the deadly atom, yet both racing to alter that uncertain balance of terror that stays the hand of mankind's final war.

So let us begin anew – remembering on both sides that civility is not a sign of weakness, and sincerity is always subject to proof. Let us never negotiate out of fear. But let us never fear to negotiate.

Let both sides explore what problems unite us instead of belaboring those problems which divide us. Let both sides, for the first time, formulate serious and precise proposals for the inspection and control of arms – and bring the absolute power to destroy other nations under the absolute control of all nations.

Let both sides seek to invoke the wonders of science instead of its terrors. Together let us explore the stars, conquer the deserts, eradicate disease, tap the ocean depths, and encourage the arts and commerce.

Let both sides unite to heed in all corners of the earth the command of Isaiah – to 'undo the heavy burdens and to let the oppressed go free'.

And if a beachhead of cooperation may push back the jungle of suspicion, let both sides join in a new endeavor – not a new balance of power, but a new world of law, where the strong are just and the weak secure and the peace preserved.

All this will not be finished in the first one hundred days. Nor will it be finished in the first one thousand days, nor in the life of this administration, nor even perhaps in our lifetime on this planet. But let us begin.

In your hands, my fellow citizens, more than mine, will rest the final success or failure of our course. Since this country was founded, each generation of Americans has been summoned to give testimony to its national loyalty. The graves of young Americans who answered the call to service surround the globe.

Now the trumpet summons us again – not as a call to bear arms, though arms we need – not as a call to battle, though embattled we are – but a call to bear the burden of a long twilight struggle, year in and year out, 'rejoicing in hope, patient in tribulation' – a struggle against the common enemies of man: tyranny, poverty, disease, and war itself.

Can we forge against these enemies a grand and global alliance, North and South, East and West, that can assure a more fruitful life for all mankind? Will you join in that historic effort?

In the long history of the world, only a few generations have been granted the role of defending freedom in its hour of maximum danger. I do not shrink from this responsibility – I welcome it. I do not believe that any of us would exchange places with any other people or any other generation. The energy, the faith, the devotion which we bring to this endeavor will light our country and all who serve it – and the glow from that fire can truly light the world.

And so, my fellow Americans, ask not what your country can do for you – ask what you can do for your country.

My fellow citizens of the world, ask not what America will do for you, but what together we can do for the freedom of man.

Finally, whether you are citizens of America or citizens of the world, ask of us here the same high standards of strength and sacrifice which we ask of you. With a good conscience our only sure reward, with history the final judge of our deeds, let us go forth to lead the land we love, asking his blessing and his help, but knowing that here on earth God's work must truly be our own.

INSPIRATIONAL

SPEECHES

MAHATMA GANDHI (1869–1948)

India's spiritual leader, Mahatma Gandhi, advocated non-violent resistance to Britain's rule of India. He was eventually arrested and charged with sedition for articles he had written in a youth magazine. He pleaded guilty at his trial in 1922, and made the following remarks before being sentenced to six years in prison.

Non-violence is the first article of my faith. It is the last article of my faith. But I had to make my choice. I had either to submit to a system which I considered has done an irreparable harm to my country or incur the risk of the mad fury of my people bursting forth when they understood the truth from my lips. I know that my people have sometimes gone mad. I am deeply sorry for it; and I am therefore, here, to submit not to a light penalty but to the highest penalty. I do not ask for mercy. I do not plead any extenuating act. I am here, therefore, to invite and submit to the highest penalty that can be inflicted upon me for what in law is a deliberate crime and what appears to me to be the highest duty of a citizen. The only course open to you, Mr Judge, is, as I am just going to say in my statement, either to resign your post or inflict on me the severest penalty if you believe that the system and law you are assisting to administer are good for the people. I do not expect that kind of conversion. But by the time I have finished with my statement you will, perhaps, have a glimpse of what is raging within my breast to run this maddest risk which a sane man can run.

(Ghandi then read his statement to the court.)

I owe it perhaps to the Indian public and to the public in England, to placate which this prosecution is mainly taken up, that I should explain why from a staunch loyalist and cooperator I have become an uncompromising disaffectionist and non-cooperator. To the court too I should say why I plead guilty to the charge of promoting disaffection towards the Government established by law in India.

My public life began in 1893 in South Africa in troubled weather. My first contact with British authority in that country was not of a happy character. I discovered that as a man and an Indian I had no rights. On the contrary I discovered that I had no rights as a man because I was an Indian.

But I was not baffled. I thought that this treatment of Indians was an excrescence upon a system that was intrinsically and mainly good. I gave the Government my voluntary and hearty cooperation, criticizing it fully where I felt it was faulty but never wishing its destruction.

Consequently when the existence of the Empire was threatened in 1899 by the Boer challenge, I offered my services to it, raised a volunteer ambulance corps and served at several actions that took place for the relief of Ladysmith. Similarly in 1906 at the time of the Zulu revolt I raised a stretcher-bearer party and served till the end of the 'rebellion'. On both these occasion I received medals and was even mentioned in despatches. For my work in South Africa I was given by Lord Hardinge a Kaiser-I-Hind Gold Medal. When the war broke out in 1914 between England and Germany I raised a volunteer ambulance corps in London consisting of the then resident Indians in London, chiefly students. Its work was acknowledged by the authorities to be valuable. Lastly in India when a special appeal was made at the War Conference in Delhi in 1917 by Lord Chelmsford for recruits, I struggled at the cost of my health to raise a corps in Kheda and the response was being made when the hostilities ceased and orders were received that no more recruits were wanted. In all these efforts at service I was actuated by the belief that it was possible by such services to gain a status of full equality in the Empire for my countrymen.

The first shock came in the shape of the Rowlatt Act, a law designed to rob the people of all real freedom. I felt called upon to lead an intensive agitation against it. Then followed the Punjab horrors beginning with the massacre at Jallianwala Bagh and culminating in crawling orders, public floggings and other indescribable humiliations. The Punjab crime was whitewashed and most culprits went not only unpunished but remained in service and some continued to draw pensions from the Indian revenue, and in some cases were even rewarded. I saw too that not only did the reforms not mark a change of heart, but they were only a method of further draining India of her wealth and of prolonging her servitude.

I came reluctantly to the conclusion that the British connection had made India more helpless than she ever was before, politically and economically. A disarmed India has no power of resistance against any aggressor if she wanted to engage in an armed conflict with him. So much is this the case that some of our best men consider that India must take generations before she can achieve the Dominion status. She has become so poor that she has little power of resisting famines. Before the British advent, India spun and wove in her millions of cottages just the supplement she needed for adding to her meagre agricultural resources. The cottage industry, so vital for India's existence, has been ruined by incredibly heartless and inhuman processes as described by English witnesses.

Little do town-dwellers know how the semi-starved masses of Indians are slowly sinking to lifelessness. Little do they know that their miserable comfort represents the brokerage they get for the work they do for the foreign exploiter, that the profits and the brokerage are sucked from the masses. Little do they realize that the Government established by law in British India is carried on for this exploitation of the masses. No sophistry, no jugglery in figures can explain away the evidence the skeletons in many villages present to the naked eye. I have no doubt whatsoever that both England and the town-dwellers of India will have to answer, if there is a God above, for this crime against humanity which is perhaps unequalled in history. The law itself in this country has been used to serve the foreign exploiter. My unbiased examination of the Punjab Martial Law cases has led me to believe that at least ninety-five per cent of convictions were wholly bad. My experience of political cases in India leads me to the conclusion that in nine out of every ten the condemned men were totally innocent. Their crime consisted in love of their country. In ninety-nine cases out of a hundred, justice has been denied to Indians as against Europeans in the Courts of India. This is not an exaggerated picture. It is the experience of almost every Indian who has had anything to do with such cases. In my opinion the administration of the law is thus prostituted consciously or unconsciously for the benefit of the exploiter.

The greatest misfortune is that Englishmen and their Indian associates in the administration of the country do not know that they are engaged in the crime I have attempted to describe. I am satisfied that many English and Indian officials honestly believe that they are administering one of the best systems devised in the world and that India is making steady though slow progress. They do not know that a subtle but effective system of terrorism and an organized display of force on the one hand and the deprivation of all powers of retaliation or self-defence on the other have emasculated the people and induced in them the habit of simulation. This awful habit has added to the ignorance and the self-deception of the administrators. Section 124-A under which I am happily charged is perhaps the prince among the political sections of the Indian Penal Code designed to suppress the liberty of the citizen. Affection cannot be manufactured or regulated by law. If one has no affection for a person or thing one should be free to give the fullest expression to his disaffection so long as he does not contemplate, promote or incite to violence. But the section under which Mr Banker and I are charged is one under which mere promotion of disaffection is a crime. I have studied some of the cases tried under it, and I know that some of the most loved of India's patriots have been convicted under it. I consider it a privilege, therefore, to be charged under it. I have endeavoured to give in their briefest outline the reasons for my disaffection. I have no personal ill-will against any single administrator, much less can I have any disaffection towards the King's person. But I hold it to be a virtue to be disaffected towards a Government which in its totality has done more harm to India than any previous system. Indian is less manly under the British rule than she ever was before. Holding such a belief, I consider it to be a sin to have affection for the system. And it has been a precious privilege for me to be able to write what I have in the various articles tendered in evidence against me.

In fact I believe that I have rendered a service to India and England by showing in non-cooperation the way out of the unnatural state in which both are living. In my humble opinion, non-cooperation with evil is as much a duty as is cooperation with good. But in the past, non-cooperation has been deliberately expressed in violence to the evildoer. I am endeavouring to show to my countrymen that violent non-cooperation only multiplies evil and that as evil can only be sustained by violence, withdrawal of support of evil requires complete abstention from violence. Non-violence implies voluntary submission to the penalty for non-cooperation with evil. I am here, therefore, to invite and submit cheerfully to the highest penalty that can be inflicted upon me for what in law is deliberate crime and what appears to me to be the highest duty of a citizen. The only course open to you, the Judge and the Assessors, is either to resign your posts and thus dissociate yourselves from evil if you feel that the law you are called upon to administer is an evil and that in reality I am innocent, or to inflict on me the severest penalty if you believe that the system and the law you are assisting to administer are good for the people of this country and that my activity is therefore injurious to the public weal.

MARTIN LUTHER KING (1929–1968)

One of the most inspirational leaders in history, Martin Luther King campaigned for an end to segregation in America. His 'I have a dream . . .' speech at the March on Washington for Jobs and Freedom in 1963 is one of the most stirring and memorable speeches in history. Ten months later, the Civil Rights Act was finally passed.

I am happy to join with you today in what will go down in history as the greatest demonstration for freedom in the history of our nation.

Five score years ago, a great American, in whose symbolic shadow we stand signed the Emancipation Proclamation. This momentous decree came as a great beacon light of hope to millions of Negro slaves who had been seared in the flames of withering injustice. It came as a joyous daybreak to end the long night of captivity.

But one hundred years later, we must face the tragic fact that the Negro is still not free. One hundred years later, the life of the Negro is still sadly crippled by the manacles of segregation and the chains of discrimination. One hundred years later, the Negro lives on a lonely island of poverty in the midst of a vast ocean of material prosperity. One hundred years later, the Negro is still languishing in the corners of American society and finds himself an exile in his own land. So we have come here today to dramatize an appalling condition.

In a sense we have come to our nation's capital to cash a check. When the architects of our republic wrote the magnificent words of the Constitution and the Declaration of Independence, they were signing a promissory note to which every American was to fall heir. This note was a promise that all men would be guaranteed the inalienable rights of life, liberty, and the pursuit of happiness.

It is obvious today that America has defaulted on this promissory note insofar as her citizens of color are concerned. Instead of honoring this sacred obligation, America has given the Negro people a bad check which has come back marked 'insufficient funds'.

But we refuse to believe that the bank of justice is bankrupt. We refuse to believe that there are insufficient funds in the great vaults of opportunity of this nation. So we have come to cash this check – a check that will give us upon demand the riches of freedom and the security of justice.

We have also come to this hallowed spot to remind America of the fierce urgency of now. This is no time to engage in the luxury of cooling off or to take the tranquillizing drug of gradualism.

Now is the time to rise from the dark and desolate valley of segregation to the sunlit path of racial justice. Now is the time to open the doors of opportunity to all of God's children. Now is the time to lift our nation from the quicksands of racial injustice to the solid rock of brotherhood.

It would be fatal for the nation to overlook the urgency of the moment and to underestimate the determination of the Negro. This sweltering summer of the Negro's legitimate discontent will not pass until there is an invigorating autumn of freedom and equality. Nineteen sixty-three is not an end, but a beginning. Those who hope that the Negro needed to blow off steam and will now be content will have a rude awakening if the nation returns to business as usual.

There will be neither rest nor tranquillity in America until the Negro is granted his citizenship rights.

The whirlwinds of revolt will continue to shake the foundations of our nation until the bright day of justice emerges.

But there is something that I must say to my people who stand on the warm threshold which leads into the palace of justice. In the process of gaining our rightful place we must not be guilty of wrongful deeds. Let us not seek to satisfy our thirst for freedom by drinking from the cup of bitterness and hatred.

We must forever conduct our struggle on the high place of dignity and discipline. We must not allow our creative protest to degenerate into physical violence. Again and again we must rise to the majestic heights of meeting physical force with soul force.

The marvelous new militancy which has engulfed the Negro community must not lead us to distrust of all white people, for many of our white brothers, as evidenced by their presence here today, have come to realize that their destiny is tied up with our destiny and their freedom is inextricably bound to our freedom.

We cannot walk alone. And as we walk, we must make the pledge that we shall march ahead. We cannot turn back. There are those who are asking the devotees of civil rights, 'When will you be satisfied?'

We can never be satisfied as long as our bodies, heavy with the fatigue of travel, cannot gain lodging in the motels of the highways and the hotels of the cities. We cannot be satisfied as long as the Negro's basic mobility is from a smaller ghetto to a larger one. We can never be satisfied as long as a Negro in Mississippi cannot vote and a Negro in New York believes he has nothing for which to vote.

No, no, we are not satisfied, and we will not be satisfied until justice rolls down like waters and righteousness like a mighty stream.

I am not unmindful that some of you have come here out of great trials and tribulations. Some of you have come fresh from narrow cells. Some of you have come from areas where your quest for freedom left you battered by the storms of persecution and staggered by the winds of police brutality. You have been the veterans of creative suffering. Continue to work with the faith that unearned suffering is redemptive.

Go back to Mississippi, go back to Alabama, go back to South Carolina, go back to Georgia, go back to Louisiana, go back to the slums and ghettos of our northern cities, knowing that somehow this situation can and will be changed. Let us not wallow in the valley of despair.

I say to you today, my friends, that in spite of the difficulties and frustrations of the moment, I still have a dream.

It is a dream deeply rooted in the American dream.

I have a dream that one day this nation will rise up and live out the true meaning of its creed: 'We hold these truths to be self-evident, that all men are created equal.' I have a dream that one day on the red hills of Georgia the sons of former slaves and the sons of former slave owners will be able to sit down together at a table of brotherhood. I have a dream that one day even the state of Mississippi, a desert state sweltering with the heat of injustice and oppression, will be transformed into an oasis of freedom and justice. I have a dream that my four little children will one day live in a nation where they will not be judged by the color of their skin but by the content of their character. I have a dream today. I have a dream that one day the state of Alabama, whose governor's lips are presently dripping with the words of interposition and nullification, will be transformed into a situation where little black boys and black girls will be able to join hands with little white boys and white girls and walk together as sisters and brothers. I have a dream today.

I have a dream that one day every valley shall be exalted, every hill and mountain shall be made low, the rough places will be made plain, and the crooked places will be made straight, and the glory of the Lord shall be revealed, and all flesh shall see it together.

This is our hope. This is the faith with which I return to the South. With this faith we will be able to hew out of the mountain of despair a stone of hope. With this faith we will be able to transform the jangling discords of our nation into a beautiful symphony of brotherhood. With this faith we will be able to work together, to pray together, to struggle together, to go to jail together, to stand up for freedom together, knowing that we will be free one day.

This will be the day when all of God's children will be able to sing with a new meaning, 'My country, 'tis of thee, sweet land of liberty, of thee I sing. Land where my fathers died, land of the pilgrim's pride, from every mountainside, let freedom ring.'

And if America is to be a great nation this must become true. So let freedom ring from the prodigious hilltops of New Hampshire. Let freedom ring from the mighty mountains of New York. Let freedom ring from the heightening

Alleghenies of Pennsylvania! Let freedom ring from the snowcapped Rockies of Colorado! Let freedom ring from the curvaceous peaks of California! But not only that; let freedom ring from Stone Mountain of Georgia! Let freedom ring from Lookout Mountain of Tennessee! Let freedom ring from every hill and every molehill of Mississippi. From every mountainside, let freedom ring.

When we let freedom ring, when we let it ring from every village and every hamlet, from every state and every city, we will be able to speed up that day when all of God's children, black men and white men, Jews and Gentiles, Protestants and Catholics, will be able to join hands and sing the words of the old Negro spiritual, 'Free at last! Free at last! Thank God Almighty, we are free at last!'

NELSON MANDELA (1918-)

Nelson Mandela has become a worldwide symbol of
resistance against oppression. He has spent his life fighting
against apartheid and discrimination in South Africa, and
served 27 years as a political prisoner for his beliefs. His
resilience, passion and unwavering determination moved
the world in this speech, made on his eventual release from
prison in 1990.

Friends, Comrades and fellow South Africans. I greet you all in the name of peace, democracy and freedom for all. I stand here before you not as a prophet but as a humble servant of you, the people. Your tireless and heroic sacrifices have made it possible for me to be here today. I therefore place the remaining years of my life in your hands . . .

Today the majority of South Africans, black and white, recognize that apartheid has no future. It has to be ended by our own decisive mass action in order to build peace and security. The mass campaign of defiance and other actions of our organization and people can only culminate in the establishment of democracy.

The apartheid destruction on our subcontinent is incalculable. The fabric of family life of millions of my people has been shattered. Millions are homeless and unemployed. Our economy lies in ruins and our people are embroiled in political strife.

Our resort to the armed struggle in 1960 with the formation of the military wing of the ANC, Umkhonto we Sizwe (Spear of the Nation), was a purely defensive action against the violence of apartheid. The factor which necessitated the armed struggle still exists today. We have no option but to continue . . .

Negotiations on the dismantling of apartheid will have to address the overwhelming demand of our people for a democratic, non-racial and unitary South Africa.

There must be an end to white monopoly on political power, and a fundamental restructuring of our political and economic systems to ensure that the inequalities of apartheid are addressed and our society thoroughly democratized.

It must be added that Mr de Klerk himself is a man of integrity, who is acutely aware of the dangers of a public figure not honouring his undertakings. But as an organization, we base our policy and strategy on the harsh reality we are faced with. And this reality is that we are still suffering under the policies of the Nationalist government.

Our struggle has reached a decisive moment. We call on our people to seize this moment, so that the process towards democracy is rapid and uninterrupted.

We have waited too long for our freedom! We can no longer wait. Now is the time to intensify the struggle on all fronts. To relax our efforts now would be a mistake which generations to come will not be able to forgive. The sight of freedom looming on the horizon should encourage us to redouble our efforts. It is only through disciplined mass action that our victory can be assured.

We call on our white compatriots to join us in the shaping of a new South Africa. The freedom movement is a political home for you, too. We call on the international community to continue the campaign to isolate the apartheid regime. To lift sanctions now would be to run the risk of aborting the process towards the complete eradication of apartheid.

Our march to freedom is irreversible. We must not allow fear to stand in our way. Universal suffrage on a common voters' roll in a united, democratic and non-racial South Africa is the only way to peace and racial harmony.

In conclusion I wish to go to my own words during my trial in 1964. They are as true today as they were then. I quote:

'I have fought against white domination and I have fought against black domination. I have cherished the ideal of a democratic and free society in which all persons live together in harmony and with equal opportunity. It is an ideal which I hope to live for and to achieve. But if needs be, it is an ideal for which I am prepared to die. *Amandla* (power)!'

AUSTRALIAN

SPEECHES

PETER LALOR (1827-1889)

Dissatisfied with the high cost of mining licences, diggers on the Ballarat goldfields in 1854 formed a coucil-of-war and gathered under the 'Southern Cross' flag to fight for their rights. Peter Lalor led what has come to be called the Eureka rebellion, and made this speech on his election as commander of the rebels.

Gentlemen, I find myself in the responsible position I now occupy, for this reason. The diggers, outraged at the unaccountable conduct of the Camp officials in such a wicked licence-hunt at the point of the bayonet, as the one of this morning, took it as an insult to their manhood, and a challenge to the determination come to at the monster meeting of yesterday.

The diggers rushed to their tents for arms, and crowded on Bakery-hill. They wanted a leader. No one came forward, and confusion was the consequence. I mounted the stump, where you saw me, and called on the people to 'fall in' into divisions, according to the fire-arms they had got, and to choose their own captains out of the best men they had among themselves. My call was answered with unanimous acclamation, and complied to with willing obedience.

The result, is that I have been able to bring about that order, without which it would be folly to face the pending struggle like men. I make no pretensions to military knowledge. I have not the presumption to assume the chief command, no more than any other man who means well in the cause of the diggers. I shall be glad to see the best among us take the lead. In fact, gentlemen, I expected some one who is really well known [J. B. Humffray?]* to come forward and direct our movement! However, if you appoint me your commander-in-chief, I shall not shrink; I mean to do my duty as a man. I tell you, gentlemen, if once I pledge my hand to the diggers, I will neither defile it, with treachery, nor render it contemptible by cowardice.

* J. B. Humffray was the leader of the Ballarat Reform League.

CAROLINE CHISHOLM (1808–1877)

*During the days of the gold rush, Caroline Chisholm
campaigned tirelessly on behalf of women and immigrant
families living in the Australian colonies. She encouraged
immigration and aimed to create a civilised nation. An
outspoken woman (a rarity at the time), Chisholm made
this plea to gold-diggers about their families left behind
in 1854.*

Mr Chairman, Ladies and Gentlemen, a cup of tea is always
exceedingly pleasant and refreshing, and the one which I
have been invited to partake of this evening, is particularly
agreeable to me. I can assure you that I am deeply grateful for it. (Cheers.) I am sure you would not have been
here this evening if what I have done had not met with
your approval, and I hope that what I shall yet do, may
receive your support. (Cheers.) Those whose domestic
duty it is to get a cup of tea ready – as we ladies of the col-
ony have to do – know the troubles and difficulties which
such an undertaking involves – (Laughter) and my friend
Mr Hitchcock in preparing the one of which we have just
partaken, seems, from the explanation he has given, to have
encountered his share.

It is, my friends, a glorious thing to live in a country and
amidst a people who will not allow slander of any kind on
account of religion, who will have nothing but open truth.
If I could not stand a little sifting, I should not have come
to the diggings. (Laughter and applause.) My character is
precious and valuable to me; I hope it is even more so unto

my children; and I attach some importance to it as being of some value to you. (Much applause.) And if I am jealous of my reputation it is because I feel that without character I cannot possess public confidence, and without public confidence I cannot effect any public good. Thus the sifting which I have had is a safeguard and protection, and keeps from me those who would be advocates only in words. (Applause.) Moneymaking is no part of my business. If it was, I believe I could make a fortune in many ways. During my present trip, I learnt many little ways for making money for others, but saw nothing suitable for myself. I feel there is a certain amount of work for me to do, and that I must go on, entertaining not the slightest dread for the future. Some say that I have not been sending a sufficient number of good persons to the colonies. I should like to ask those objectors if they ever did anything to help me? (Applause.) No; you will not find among the grumblers the workers. (Laughter.) I know that from experience.

It is, however, right that I should explain to you why I am here. During my fourteen years labour I have gained among a certain class a reputation for speaking truth. I may err in judgment but not in intention. Numbers are constantly applying to me for advice, but I never seek to lead them upon the opinions of others: the rule I have always observed has been, never to go by what I hear, but to judge only from what I see. (Applause.) Consequently when many persons in Melbourne were inquiring of me, 'Shall I go to the diggings?' 'Would you advise me to go up the country?' I felt the responsibility of my position, as, if I advised them to go, and anything went wrong with them, they would blame me. My reply has invariably been, 'As soon as I can make arrangements, I shall go to the diggings, and then I will tell you.' I have delayed this for some time, though I have been under a promise, made in England, to visit the diggings.

The mission I am on is a sacred one. I have promised parents to go in search of their children – I have promised wives to make inquiries for their husbands – I have promised sisters to seek their brothers, and friends to look for friends – and oh! let me ask and implore you who have left friends at home, if you have been neglectful of your first duty, if, in your lust for gold, or in the pursuit of business, you have not written to those you have left behind, to go home this night and do your duty. Let them, too, taste of the fruits of your labors. They might be in need of your assistance. You may have left them in comfort and security, and do not think of the change that may have occurred. For they are liable to change when the strong arm that has been their natural support is withdrawn from them. Whatever their condition they must be anxious to hear from you, to know whether you are alive or not.

In a first journey like this, it is important to make all the arrangements that are contemplated. Still a great deal may be done – much good may be effected with present means, and if it is attempted, you will not only have me in Castlemaine again, but again and again. (Applause.) I shall look for you to work your own district well, and act in unison with others. I shall then have a great number of agents to help me in carrying out my objects.

The husbands who have left their wives at home, will find that I shall follow them. (Laughter and applause.) There are many of them about the diggings. The other day, as I was passing along, a digger whom I approached gave a sudden start, and said, 'That's Mrs Chisholm!' I acknowledged my identity. 'Oh,' he said, 'I never thought of sending for my wife until I saw you.' Now for two years had that man been digging at Castlemaine – dig, dig, digging, and yet, as he assured me, had never thought of sending for his wife until he saw me. (Cries of 'shame upon him'.) There is a great number like him – equally forgetful. Now, with me as a reminder, with two or three gentlemen in Castlemaine working with me, and co-operating with a committee in England, we should soon find out these careless husbands. Will you do all you can to help me? I am sure the females will. I think the married men will. If the single men do not help me, I will not help them. (Laughter and applause.)

When I was in New South Wales, I thought nothing of a journey of 100 miles. I knew that I could depend upon the hospitality of the people on the line of road, to meet any want on the part of myself and the persons with me. But I was afraid, when some persons proposed to accompany me on the present occasion, that we should not meet with accommodation on the road. There is a great difference between buying a cart at fifty guineas and getting one at eleven guineas; and I had to wait till I could make things convenient. I had a pair of horses lent to me, and started on my journey.

At a public party a few days before, I met his Excellency the Lieutenant Governor. He had been informed of my intended visit to the goldfields, expressed a great desire that I should start without delay, and said he was exceedingly anxious to hear what I thought of them. My mission was known to be a domestic one; still, when I was leaving, two or three officials furnished me with letters of introduction; I had, besides, a kind of general letter, in which, in the event of my requiring any assistance, the officials on the goldfields were requested to pay me the necessary attention. Well, I did get into trouble. I broke my shaft. (Laughter.) I made use of the note, and the escort cart was lent to me until my own was repaired. (Applause.) I did not find it necessary to use my letters of introduction; for, to use the expression of my friend, Mr Hitchcock, my object was to 'sift' the diggings, to look into the domestic wants of the diggers, and see what could be done to provide them with comfortable, happy homes. (Applause.)

We have been told that the health of the Queen was drunk in this hall with 'nine times nine and one cheer more'; but what a cheer would the diggers give if the homes they go to at night were something better than the blankets under which they have to creep like dogs. Give them good homes, and if the Russians came tomorrow, the diggers would all turn out and fight in their defence like men. (Applause.) No man knows the strength of his arm until he raises it to defend his wife or protect his children. (Applause.) I was told at Bendigo that if I stayed a little while there, I should receive a large number of diggers' grievances. That is not a part of my mission. I am looking after their rights; they will have an expensive commission to redress their grievances. (Applause.) Numbers have complained to me very grievously of many things which they feel to press on them heavily; but I do not feel much sympathy or much pity for any body of men who pay so little respect to their own sex as to live without wives when they can so well afford to maintain them. (Laughter.) If I had power to do so, I would relieve of taxes all the married men, and give a bounty on all the women and children introduced into the diggers' districts. (Applause and laughter.)

The diggers have great grievances, but they are not competent to decide upon the remedy. It is impossible for them to act with discretion and judgement, huddled together, as they are, in fifties, listening to the evil agitator. It will be when they are really at home, with their wives and families – when they live in peace and quietness, that they will be best able to tell what they want. Then, when they can take care of the inside of their homes, and feel that the outside is protected by police, no longer regarded as an evil, their influence will be legitimately exercised. (Applause.)

The difficulties that impede the reunion of wives with their husbands have been much exaggerated by the men themselves. I know a case in which a man, writing home to his wife, and sending her no money, said he had met with an accident – that a tree had fallen upon him and broken his leg. Another letter narrated another fracture, and in the course of one day I have seen five different letters, each alleging fractured limbs, and written by men who, unlike the man who never thought about his wife, were thinking how to excuse themselves for not sending their partners any money. (Laughter and applause.)

Now I do not think so much of this would happen if the diggers had any place where they might safely deposit their gold. I think it would be a very good thing if savings banks could be established here. It might easily be done. I have no doubt that we should hear of sons sending to parents, and husbands to wives, much more frequently than at present, if they could save their money. I think that some institution of the nature of a savings bank could be attached to the Gold Commissioners' departments. There is another point, too, on which, I think, the service of the Commissioners could be made useful – that is, in giving information to people who wish to purchase lands in their respective districts. I should be glad if any gentleman would aid me in carrying this latter point out. Great good would result from it. I am constantly applied to by men with families, and perhaps £200 or £300 in cash, who want to get on land of their own. To such men the opportunity of applying to the Commissioners, and obtaining the knowledge they require, would be a great advantage.

With reference to the introduction of females here – unless the ladies of the district will come forward and co-operate in protecting those who are sent here, so that those who are good may be saved from becoming bad, it will be useless to attempt it. If you wish to prosper in this district you must encourage population; and take advantage of the present time, for it will be long before there will be a better. Wages are higher in England, and fewer people are coming out; and the love of the land is so strong among those you have here, that if you do not speedily find some for them, they will dig your gold and carry it away. (Much applause.) I know many girls get into difficulties through being discharged from one place before they have another to go to. They seek temporary lodgings, are exposed to temptations, and generally the more innocent the girl the sooner she falls. I shall be happy to do what I can to send girls here when I know that the ladies of Castlemaine are ready to perform their part. (Applause.)

Taking the general character of the diggers of this place, I believe that anything like ordinary care and supervision over females who may arrive here, would result in good. Where there is one man among them who will annoy a respectable female, there will be found ten to protect her. (Applause.) But there must be a Home, founded in the spirit of true Christian liberty that we all love and venerate. If, then, you will, in your district, found such a Home, I will do all I can to fill it. (Applause.) I mention this with especial reference to wives and families.

I have been informed that in this district alone there are £70,000 deposited with government, being the property of diggers; so that there does appear to be a sort of savings bank here already. But the money is yielding no interest – that would keep me awake all night! (Laughter and applause.) It belongs to working men, and ought to be worked. Government may well be short of money. I hope some of this large amount will be soon withdrawn by the working men who have placed it there, and their wives sent for. In the meantime, let them know where they may obtain lands to settle and build their own cottages on – that is an object I will arrange and forward to the utmost of my power. Just as I would endeavour to procure for you a supply of female servants to lead them into marriage, so I recommend men to dig for gold, wherewith to purchase lands and settle. (Applause. – A communication was here made to Mrs Chisholm by Mr Hitchcock.)

I have much satisfaction in telling you that it is intended to establish, in Castlemaine, a branch of the Melbourne savings bank! (Applause.)

EDMUND BARTON (1849–1920)

Australia's first prime minister, Edmund Barton was central to the push for Federation – trained as a lawyer, he helped to draft the Federal constitution. In 1903, he made this speech to parliament, arguing that when it came to defense of the nation, Australia would have to continue to rely on Britain for protection.

Let us call ourselves Britons. In using the term Britons in Australia, I wish it to be as clear as possible that, in my belief, we have not forfeited, by our emigration, or by that of our fathers, any of the rights of Britishers at home, or any of our share in either the glory or the material prosperity of the Empire. We are Britons of the Empire. We did not sever ourselves from the rest of the Empire when we came here, neither did the fathers of those of us, who like myself are natives of the soil, do so. We retain our heritage, and with it our responsibilities. We cannot have the one, and say 'no' to the other, because the thing is impossible, and because we should be poor Britons if we did. Surely, the consciousness that we are at least making a small attempt towards the equalization of these burdens is 'something to show' for our expenditure.

With regard to the next objection, that the agreement does not satisfy our local aspirations, or give proper scope to our patriotism, I recognise to the full the importance of this contention, and have always endeavoured to so mould the Constitution and the legislation of the Commonwealth as to give fuller scope for the national aspirations of Australians. But this is a case where our patriotic feelings towards the Empire of which Australia forms a part must express themselves, because we regard the Empire as one for purposes of naval defence. If we do not take that view, we must accept the alternative, that the Empire must operate by scattered units, and lose the power of concentration, and its Navy be by so much the more open to defeat and capture in detail.

We must look at the great question of naval defence from the point of view of citizens of the Empire. Heaven forbid that I should ask any one to relinquish his feeling of local patriotism, or do anything which would be unjust to his fellow citizens in Australia. But we can be just to Australia and still meet our obligations to the Empire so long as we recognise them. On the day when we cease to recognise them, we should be honest, and say to the mother country, 'We want to go.' Just as we look at Federal questions as Australians rather than as citizens of the States, so we must look at questions of Empire as citizens of the Empire rather than as citizens of Australia. I do not wish to use the word 'Imperial,' because in some men's ears it carries the far-off sound of absolute despotism and domination, but we may speak of the Empire because we have no other name to give. It is an aggregation of free men in free lands, and while we belong to it we must look at questions of Empire as citizens of the Empire, just as we look at Australian questions as citizens of Australia.

If we wished to cut the painter – and no one is proposing to do so – we could rid ourselves of these obligations. But at what price? We should be independent, but we should be much more exposed to the insults and intrusions of foreign Powers than we are now, when there is a shield of protection thrown over us which has taken the Empire ages to make, and such as we could not make apart. We cannot make this ægis for ourselves, and we cannot put on ready made the garb of Empire, because we do not want the 'slop clothes' of Empire. We are, I take it, content with our position as a free self-governing portion of the Empire. We are content to maintain it at a reasonable expenditure – at an expenditure much less than we should have to make if we shared in the defence of any other Empire; and for a purpose which means this: Take one portion away from the Empire and you may as well take another. Be a party to its disintegration, even by abstention from what is right, and you make that disintegration easier. The principle surely should be this: Touch one of us and you touch us all. What was our answer when South Africa was attacked? Were we wrong in making that answer? To my dying day I shall not believe so. What was at stake? Not only perhaps the most important of the trade routes of the Empire, which provided the material solace to our action. We decided to act when it was too early to think of that, but we believed that success against England meant the disintegration of the Empire at that one point, which we thought almost as much against our interests as if some other portion of the Empire, or we ourselves, were cut off from it.

What, then, is the right principle to adopt in regard to the defence of the Empire? The principle that by common action we must keep every portion of it intact. By going on our own initiative in various directions, we leave every portion of it open to attack. I do not think that there is anything in our local aspirations which entitles us to give the lie to that principle. Our 'patriotic' feelings, if I may use a word which is sometimes derided, must find expression in our acts. We may maintain the name of our attachment to the Empire, and do nothing; but that seems to be a fair way of getting ourselves branded, not only as mean men, but as hypocrites.

Under this agreement we shall give Australia better protection than we could if we adopted the alternative of an Australian Navy, unless we went to a cost which, in our present stage, is prohibitive. There can be no want of loyalty in giving Australia adequate defence at a much lower rate than it would otherwise cost. While we remain part of the Empire, there will arise questions of Imperial rather than of local importance, and they will arise even if we turn away and shut our eyes. But it is our duty to have regard to these questions so long as we remain in the Empire, and to recognise what our position requires of us, not to the extent of slavish adherence to everything done by others, but to the extent of realizing that with participation in the advantages of the Empire comes reciprocal obligation. Holding the views we do as to the sound principle of naval defence, we are unable to subscribe to the theory that our loyalty to Australia calls upon us to set up a separate Navy.

WILLIAM MORRIS 'BILLY' HUGHES
(1862–1952)

An English migrant, William Morris Hughes was prime minister of Australia from 1915 to 1923. A staunch supporter of Britain in the First World War, Hughes encouraged Australian conscription. He made this speech to parliament in 1919, defending his actions at the international Versailles Conference, which was held to establish the terms of peace following the end of the war.

When I ask this Parliament to approve of this Treaty, I have a right, as the spokesman for Australia to speak proudly of what Australia has done through her soldiers, her sailors, and all those who have striven, each in their own way, to serve their country in its hour of peril – the women, the nurses of Australia, and those who went out to serve their country, even in the manufacture of munitions, and aid in every possible way in the great conflict which has shaken the world to its very foundations. There never was, in the history of the world before this war, a record like that of this young community of five million people. We sent out a greater Army than Great Britain herself had ever sent out before, and we transported it over 12,000 miles of ocean. We maintained five divisions of fighting men at the front line, men who will stand comparison with the finest and bravest soldiers of any of the Allied and Associated Powers. We need not claim more distinction than that. It is sufficient, if we are able to say that on the land, and on the sea, and in the air, in every theatre of war – in Europe, in Asia, in the Pacific – Australia played her part, and that, in the great victory that has been achieved, Australia has done well, or, rather, her soldiers have done well for her. They have done great things, and have given to all of us freedom and safety. They have assured to us forever the possibility of realizing all those ideals which we cherish above life itself. Only we ourselves, by being recreant to the cause for which they fought and died, can now destroy this temple of our liberties, the keys of which they have handed to us stained with their hearts' blood.

It was abundantly evident to my colleague and to myself, as well as to the representatives of other Dominions, that Australia must have separate representation at the Peace Conference. Consider the vastness of the Empire, and the diversity of interests represented. Look at it geographically, industrially, politically, or how you will, and it will be seen that no one can speak for Australia but those who speak as representatives of Australia herself. Great Britain could not, in the very nature of things, speak for us. Britain has very many interests to consider besides ours, and some of those interests do not always coincide with ours. It was necessary, therefore – and the same applies to other Dominions – that we should be represented. Not as at first suggested, in a British panel, where we would take our place in rotation, but with a separate representation like other belligerent nations. Separate and direct representation was at length conceded to Australia and to every other self-governing Dominion.

By this recognition Australia became a nation, and entered into a family of nations on a footing of equality. We had earned that, or rather, our soldiers had earned it for us. In the achievement of victory they had played their part, and no nation had a better right to be represented than Australia. This representation was vital to us, particularly when we consider that at this world Conference thirty-two nations and over a billion people were directly represented. It was a Conference of representatives of the people of the whole world, excepting only Germany, the other enemy Powers, Russia, and a few minor nations. In this world Conference, the voice of this young community of five million people had to make itself heard. In this gathering of men representing nations with diverse and clashing interests, Australia had to press her views, and to endeavour to insist upon their acceptance by other nations.

Let me give honorable members some idea of the Conference, which consisted of more than seventy delegates – about as many as there are honorable members of this Chamber – men of all colours, and from every part of the world. There were representatives from China, Japan, Liberia, Hayti, Siam, Brazil, America, Britain, India, Roumania, Poland and Greece. There were men speaking diverse tongues, and having ideals as far asunder as the poles. There were interests which had their origin in thousands of years of tradition, and in race and geographical position. Here was Australia, an outpost of the Empire, a great continent peopled by a handful of men, called upon to defend, amongst other things, a policy which could not be understood, and which was not understood, by those with whom we consorted. I speak of the policy of a White Australia. Imaging the difficulties of the position, and the clashing of warring interests; for, while the world changes, human nature remains ever the same. While there was a sincere desire to obtain a just Peace, each nation's conception of justice differed. Each nation desired what it considered necessary for its own salvation, though it might trench on the liberties, rights, or material welfare of others.

Honorable members who have travelled in the East or in Europe will be able to understand with what difficulty this world assemblage of men, gathered from all the corners of the earth – men representing four hundred million Chinese, men representing Japan, men representing India, Siam, Hayti, and Liberia; men representing partially coloured populations – were able to appreciate this ideal of those five million people who had dared to say, not only that this great continent was theirs, but that none should enter in except such as they chose. I venture to say, therefore, that perhaps the greatest thing which we have achieved, under such circumstances and in such an assemblage, is the policy of a White Australia. On this matter I know that I speak for most, if not all, of the people of Australia. There are some at the two extreme poles of political opinion who do not hold those views, but their numbers, thank God! are quite insignificant, and their influence, I hope, even less important. Remember that this is the only community in the Empire, if not, indeed, in the world, where there is so little admixture of race. Do you realize that, if you go in England from one county to another, men speak with a different accent; that if you go a few miles men speak with a different tongue; that if you go from one part of France to another, men can hardly understand one another? Yet you can go from Perth to Sydney, and from Hobart to Cape York, and find men speaking the same tongue, with the same accent. Place on that bench men from Alice Springs, Cape York, Hobart, and Adelaide, and you cannot distinguish them in speech, form, or feature. We are all of the same race, and speak the same tongue in the same way. That cannot be said of any other Dominion in the Empire, except New Zealand, where, after all, it can be said only with reservations, because that country has a large population of Maoris. We are more British than the people of Great Britain, and we hold firmly to the great principle of the White Australia, because we know what we know. We have these liberties, and we believe in our race and in ourselves, and in our capacity to achieve our great destiny, which is to hold this vast continent in trust for those of our race who come after us, and who stand with us in the battle of freedom. The White Australia is yours. You may do with it what you please; but, at any rate, the soldiers have achieved the victory, and my colleague and I have brought that great principle back to you from the Conference. Here it is, at least as safe as it was on the day when it was first adopted by this Parliament.

What has been won? If the fruits of victory are to be measured by national safety and liberty, and the high ideals for which these boys died, the sacrifice has not been in vain. They died for the safety of Australia. Australia is safe. They died for liberty, and liberty is now assured to us and to all men. They have made for themselves and their country a name that will not die.

Looking back, through the vista of years of trial, tribulation and turmoil, into that Valley of the Shadow of Death into which we and all the free peoples of the earth were plunged, we may now lift up our voices, and thank God that, through their sacrifice, we have been brought safely into the green pastures of peace.

We turn now from war to peace. We live in a new world; a world bled white by the cruel wounds of war. Victory is ours, but the price of victory is heavy. The whole earth has been shaken to its very core. Upon the foundations of victory we would build the new temple of our choice.

Industrially, socially, politically, we cannot, any more than other nations, escape the consequences of the war. The whole world lies bleeding and exhausted from the frightful struggle. There is no way of salvation, save by the gospel of work. Those who endeavour to set class against class, or to destroy wealth, are counsellors of destruction. There is hope for this free Australia of ours only if we put aside our differences, strive to emulate the deeds of those who by their valour and sacrifice have given us liberty and safety, and resolve to be worthy of them and the cause for which they fought.

JOHN CURTIN (1885–1945)

*Prime minister of Australia from 1941 to 1945, John
Curtin made the tactical judgement to support the US
government decisions, rather than British, during the Second
World War. When Darwin was bombed by the Japanese in
1942, Curtin made this broadcast to the men and women
of the US, pledging that Australians – as 'the last bastion'
between American and Japan – would give their all.*

Men and women of the United States:

I speak to you from Australia. I speak from a united
people to a united people, and my speech is aimed to
serve all the people of the nations united in the struggle to
save mankind.

On the great waters of the Pacific Ocean war now
breathes its bloody steam. From the skies of the Pacific
pours down a deadly hail. In the countless islands of the
Pacific the tide of war flows madly. For you in America; for
us in Australia, it is flowing badly.

Let me then address you as comrades in this war and tell
you a little of Australia and Australians.

I am not speaking to your Government. We have long
been admirers of Mr Roosevelt and have the greatest confidence that he understands fully the critical situation in the
Pacific and that America will go right out to meet it. For all
that America has done, both before and after entering the
war, we have the greatest admiration and gratitude.

It is to the people of America I am now speaking; to you
who are, or will be, fighting; to you who are sweating in
factories and workshops to turn out the vital munitions of

war; to all of you who are making the sacrifices in one way or another to provide the enormous resources required for our great task.

I speak to you at a time when the loss of Java and the splendid resistance of the gallant Dutch together give us a feeling of both sadness and pride. Japan has moved one step further in her speedy march south; but the fight of the Dutch and Indonese in Java has shown that a brave, freedom-loving people are more than a match for the yellow aggressor given even a shade below equality in striking and fighting weapons.

But facts are stern things. We, the allied nations, were unready. Japan, behind her wall of secrecy, had prepared for war on a scale of which neither we nor you had knowledge.

We have all made mistakes, we have all been too slow; we have all showed weakness – all the Allied Nations. This is not a time to wrangle about who has been most to blame. Now our eyes are open.

The Australian Government has fought for its people. We never regarded the Pacific as a segment of the great struggle. We did not insist that it was a primary theatre of war, but we did say, and events have so far, unhappily, proved us right, that the loss of the Pacific can be disastrous.

Who, among us, contemplating the future on that day in December last when Japan struck like an assassin at Pearl Harbor, at Manila, at Wake and Guam, would have hazarded a guess that by March the enemy would be astride all the south-west Pacific except General Macarthur's gallant men, and Australia and New Zealand?

But that is the case. And, realising very swiftly that it would be the case, the Australian Government sought a full and proper recognition of the part the Pacific was playing in the general strategic disposition of the world's warring forces.

It was, therefore, but natural that, within 20 days after Japan's first treacherous blow, I said on behalf of the Australian Government that we looked to America as the paramount factor on the democracies' side in the Pacific.

There is no belittling of the Old Country in this outlook. Britain has fought and won in the air the tremendous battle of Britain. Britain has fought, and with your strong help, has won the equally vital battle of the Atlantic. She has a paramount obligation to supply all possible help to Russia. She cannot, at the same time, go all out in the Pacific. We, with New Zealand, represent Great Britain here in the Pacific – we are her sons – and on us the responsibility falls. I pledge you my word we will not fail. You, as I have said, must be our leader. We will pull knee to knee with you for every ounce of our weight.

We look to America, among other things, for counsel and advice and therefore it is our wish that the Pacific War Council should be located at Washington. It is a matter of some regret to us that, even now, after 95 days of Japan's staggering advance south, ever south, we have not obtained first-hand contact with America.

Therefore, we propose sending to you our Minister for External affairs (Dr H. V. Evatt), who is no stranger to your country, so that we may benefit from his discussions with your authorities. Dr Evatt's wife, who will accompany him, was born in the United States.

Dr Evatt will not go to you as a mendicant. He will go to you as the representative of a people as firmly determined to hold and hit back at the enemy as courageously as those people from whose loins we spring – those people who withstood the disaster of Dunkirk, the fury of Goering's blitz, the shattering blows of the Battle of the Atlantic. He will go to tell you that we are fighting mad; that our people have a government that is governing with orders and not with weak-kneed suggestions; that we Australians are a people who, while somewhat inexperienced and uncertain as to what war on their soil may mean, are nevertheless ready for anything, and will trade punches, giving odds if needs be, until we rock the enemy back on his heels.

We are then committed, heart and soul, to total warfare. How far, you may ask me, have we progressed along that road?

I may answer you this way. Out of every ten men in Australia, four are now wholly engaged in war as members of the fighting forces or making the munitions and equipment to fight with. The other six, besides feeding and clothing the whole ten and their families, have to produce the food and wool and metal which Britain needs for her very existence.

We are not, of course, stopping at four out of ten. We had over three when Japan challenged our life and liberty. The proportion is now growing every day. On the one hand we are ruthlessly cutting out unessential expenditure so as to free men and women for war work; and on the other, mobilizing woman power to the utmost to supplement the men. From four out of ten devoted to war, we shall pass to five and six out of ten. We have no limits.

We have no qualms here. There is no fifth column in this country. We are all the one race – the English-speaking race. We will not yield easily a yard of our soil. We have great space here and tree by tree, village by village, and town by town we will fall back if we must. That will occur only if we lack the means of meeting the enemy with parity in materials and machines.

For, remember, we are the Anzac breed. Our men stormed Gallipoli; they swept through the Libyan desert; they were the 'rats' of Tobruk; they were the men who fought under 'bitter, sarcastic, pugnacious Gordon Bennett' down Malaya and were still fighting when the surrender of Singapore came.

These men gave of their best in Greece and Crete; they will give more than their best on their own soil, where their hearths and homes lie under enemy threat.

Our air force are in the Kingsford-Smith tradition. You have, no doubt, met quite a lot of them in Canada; the Nazis have come to know them at Hamburg and Berlin and in paratroop landings in France.

Our naval forces silently do their share on the seven seas.

I am not boasting to you. But were I to say less I would not be paying proper due to a band of men who have been tested in the crucible of world wars and hallmarked as pure metal.

Our fighting forces are born attackers; we will hit the enemy wherever we can, as often as we can, and the extent of it will be measured only by the weapons to our hands.

Dr Evatt will tell you that Australia is a nation stripped for war. Our minds are set on attack rather than defence. We believe in fact that attack is the best defence; here in the Pacific it is the only defence. We know it means risks, but 'safety first' is the devil's catchword today.

Business interests in Australia are submitting with a good grace to iron control and drastic elimination of profits. Our great Labour unions are accepting the suspension of rights and privileges which have been sacred for two generations, and are submitting to an equally iron control of the activities of their members. It is now 'work or fight' for everyone in Australia.

The Australian Government has so shaped its policy that there will be a place for every citizen in the country. There are three means of service – in the fighting forces; in the labour forces; in the essential industries. For the first time in the history of this country a complete call-up, or draft, as you refer to it in America, has been made.

I say to you, as a comfort to our friends and a stiff warning to our enemies, that only the infirm remain outside the compass of our war plans.

We fight with what we have and what we have is our all. We fight for the same free institutions that you enjoy. We fight so that, in the words of Lincoln, 'government of the people, for the people, by the people, shall not perish from the earth'. Our legislature is elected the same as is yours; and we will fight for it, and for the right to have it, just as you will fight to keep the Capital at Washington the meeting place of freely-elected men and women representative of a free people.

But I give you this warning: Australia is the last bastion between the West Coast of America and the Japanese. If Australia goes, the Americas are wide open.

It is said that the Japanese will by-pass Australia and that they can be met and routed in India. I say to you that the saving of Australia is the saving of America's west coast.

If you believe anything to the contrary then you delude yourselves.

Be assured of the calibre of our national character. This war may see the end of much that we have painfully and slowly built in our 150 years of existence. But even though all of it go, there will still be Australians fighting on Australian soil until the turning point be reached, and we will advance over blackened ruins, through blasted and fire-swept cities, across scorched plains, until we drive the enemy into the sea.

I give you the pledge of my country. There will always be an Australian Government and there will always be an Australian people. We are too strong in our hearts; our spirit is too high; the justice of our cause throbs too deeply in our being for that high purpose to be overcome.

I may be looking down a vista of weary months; of soul-shaking reverses; of grim struggle; of back-breaking work. But as surely as I sit here talking to you across the war-tossed Pacific Ocean I see our flag; I see Old Glory; I see the proud banner of the heroic Chinese; I see the standard of the valiant Dutch.

And I see them flying high in the wind of liberty over a Pacific from which aggression has been wiped out; over peoples restored to freedom; and flying triumphant as the glorified symbols of united nations strong in will and in power to achieve decency and dignity, unyielding to evil in any form.

GOUGH WHITLAM (1916–)

Labor prime minister of Australia from 1972 to 1975,
Gough Whitlam was dedicated to generating reform. In
particular, he acknowledged the need to create legislation
for Aboriginal land rights. This 1975 speech celebrated the
formal transfer of the Crown lease of the Gurindji ancestral
lands to Vincent Lingiari, the traditional owner.

On this great day, I, Prime Minister of Australia, speak to you on behalf of the people of Australia – all Australians who honour the land that we live in.

For them I want:

First, to congratulate you and those who have shared your struggle on the victory you have won in that fight for justice begun nine years ago when in protest you walked off Wave Hill Station;

Secondly, to acknowledge that we Australians have still much to do to redress the injustice and oppression that has for so long been the lot of black Australians;

Thirdly, to promise you that this act of restitution which we perform today will not stand alone – your fight was not for yourselves alone and we are determined that Aboriginal Australians everywhere will be helped by it;

Fourthly, to promise that, through their government, the people of Australia will help you in your plans to use this land for the Gurindji;

Finally, to give back to you formally in Aboriginal and Australian law ownership of this land of your fathers.

Vincent Lingiari, I solemnly hand you these deeds as proof, in Australian law, that these lands belong to the Gurindji people and I put into your hands this piece of earth itself as a sign we restore them to you and your children forever.

Just three months later, the Senate refused to pass Labor's proposed budget and the Governor General, Sir John Kerr, responded by sacking Whitlam and ordering a federal election.Whitlam gave this angry reponse to his dismissal on 11 November 1975.

Well may we say 'God Save the Queen', because nothing will save the Governor-General! The proclamation which you have just heard read by the Governor-General's official secretary was countersigned 'Malcolm Fraser' who will undoubtedly go down in Australian history from Remembrance Day 1975 as Kerr's cur. They won't silence the outskirts of Parliament House, even if the inside has been silenced for the next few weeks. The Governor-General's proclamation was signed after he already made an appointment to meet the Speaker at a quarter to five. The House of Representatives had requested the Speaker to give the Governor-General its decision that Mr Fraser did not have the confidence of the House and that the Governor-General should call me to form the Government.

Maintain your rage and enthusiasm through the campaign for the election now to be held and until polling day.

PAUL KEATING (1944-)

*Paul Keating was prime minister from 1991 to 1996,
during which time the historic Mabo judgement was passed,
defining the rights of traditional land owners. Keating
made this groundbreaking, empathetic speech in Redfern
on 10 December 1992, at the launch of the Year for
Indigenous People.*

Ladies and gentlemen:

I am very pleased to be here today at the launch of
Australia's celebration of the 1993 International Year of the
World's Indigenous People. It will be a year of great significance for Australia. It comes at a time when we have
committed ourselves to succeeding in the test which so
far we have always failed. Because, in truth, we cannot
confidently say that we have succeeded as we would like
to have succeeded if we have not managed to extend
opportunity and care, dignity and hope to the indigenous
people of Australia – the Aboriginal and Torres Straight
Island people.

This is a *fundamental* test of our social goals and our
national will: our ability to say to ourselves and the rest of
the world that Australia *is* a first rate social democracy, that
we are what we should be – *truly* the land of the fair go and
the better chance.

There is no more basic test of how seriously we mean
these things. It is a test of our self-knowledge. Of how
well we know the land we live in. How well we know our
history. How well we recognise the fact that, complex as
our contemporary identity is, it cannot be separated from

Aboriginal Australia. How well we know what Aboriginal Australians know about Australia.

Redfern is a good place to contemplate these things. Just a mile or two from the place where the first European settlers landed, in too many ways it tells us that their failure to bring much more than devastation and demoralisation to Aboriginal Australia continues to be our failure. More I think than most Australians recognise, the plight of Aboriginal Australians affects us all. In Redfern it might be tempting to think that the reality Aboriginal Australians face is somehow contained here, and that the rest of us are insulated from it. But or course, while the dilemmas may exist here, they are far from contained. We know the same dilemmas and more are faced all over Australia.

That is perhaps the point of this Year of the World's Indigenous People: to bring the dispossessed out of the shadows, to recognise that they are part of us, and that we cannot give indigenous Australians up without giving up many of our own most deeply held values, much of our own identity – and our own humanity. Nowhere in the world, I would venture, is the message more stark than it is in Australia.

We simply cannot sweep injustice aside. Even if our own conscience allowed us to, I am sure, that in due course, the world and the people of our region would not. There should be no mistake about this – our success in resolving these issues will have a significant bearing on our standing in the world. However intractable the problems seem, we cannot resign ourselves to failure – any more than we can hide behind the contemporary version of Social Darwinism which says that to reach back for the poor and dispossessed is to risk being dragged down. That seems to me not only morally indefensible, but bad history.

We non-Aboriginal Australians should perhaps remind ourselves that Australia once reached out for us. Didn't Australia provide opportunity and care for the dispossessed Irish? The poor of Britain? The refugees from war and famine and persecution in the countries of Europe and Asia? Isn't it reasonable to say that if we can build a prosperous and remarkably harmonious multicultural society in Australia, surely we can find just solutions to the problems which beset the first Australians – the people to whom the most injustice has been done.

And, as I say, the starting point might be to recognise that the problem starts with us non-Aboriginal Australians.

It *begins*, I think, with that act of recognition. Recognition that it was we who did the dispossessing.

We took the traditional lands and smashed the traditional way of life.

We brought the diseases. The alcohol.

We committed the murders.

We took the children from their mothers.

We practised discrimination and exclusion.

It was *our* ignorance and *our* prejudice.

And *our* failure to imagine these things being done to us.

With some noble exceptions, we failed to make the most basic human response and enter into their hearts and minds.

We failed to ask – how would I feel if this was done to me?

As a consequence, we failed to see that what we were doing degraded all of us.

If we needed a reminder of this, we received it this year. The Report of the Royal Commission into Aboriginal Deaths in Custody showed with devastating clarity that the past lives on in inequality, racism and injustice. In the prejudice and ignorance of non-Aboriginal Australians, and in the demoralisation and desperation, the fractured identity, of so many Aborigines and Torres Strait Islanders.

For all this, I do not believe that the report should fill us with guilt. Down the years, there has been no shortage of guilt, but it has not produced the responses we need. Guilt is not a very constructive emotion. I think what we need to do is open our hearts a bit. All of us. Perhaps when we recognise what we have in common we will see the things which must be done – the practical things.

There is something of this in the creation of the Council for Aboriginal Reconciliation. The Council's mission is to forge a new partnership built on justice and equity and an appreciation of the heritage of Australia's indigenous people. In the abstract those terms are meaningless. We have to give meaning to 'justice' and 'equity' – and, as I have said several times this year, we will only give them meaning when we commit ourselves to achieving concrete results.

If we improve the living conditions in one town, they will improve in another. And another. If we raise the standard of health by twenty per cent one year, it will be raised more the next. If we open one door others will follow.

When we see improvement, when we see more dignity, more confidence, more happiness – we will know we are going to win. We need these practical building blocks of change.

The Mabo Judgment should be seen as one of these. By doing away with the bizarre conceit that this continent had no owners prior to the settlement of Europeans, Mabo establishes a fundamental truth and lays the basis for justice. It will be much easier to work from that basis than has ever been the case in the past. For that reason alone we should ignore the isolated outbreaks of hysteria and hostility of the past few months. Mabo is an historic decision – we can make it an historic *turning point*, the basis of a new relationship between indigenous and non-Aboriginal Australians.

The message should be that there is nothing to fear or to lose in the recognition of historical truth, or the extension of social justice, or the deepening of Australian social democracy to include indigenous Australians. There is everything to gain. Even the unhappy past speaks for this.

Where Aboriginal Australians have been included in the life of Australia they have made remarkable contributions. Economic contributions, particularly in the pastoral and agricultural industry. They are there in the frontier and exploration history of Australia. They are there in the wars. In sport to an extraordinary degree. In literature and art and music.

In all these things they have shaped our knowledge of this continent and of ourselves. They have shaped our identity. They are there in the Australian legend. We should never forget – they have helped build this nation. And if we have a sense of justice, as well as common sense, we will forge a new partnership.

As I said, it might help us if we non-Aboriginal Australians imagined *ourselves* dispossessed of land we had lived on for fifty thousand years – and then imagined ourselves told that it had never been ours.

Imagine if *ours* was the oldest culture in the world and we were told that it was worthless.

Imagine if *we* had resisted this settlement, suffered and died in the defence of our land, and then were told in history books that we had given up without a fight.

Imagine if non-Aboriginal Australians had served their country in peace and war and were then ignored in history books.

Imagine if *our* feats on sporting fields had inspired admiration and patriotism and yet did nothing to diminish prejudice.

Imagine if *our* spiritual life was denied and ridiculed.

Imagine if we had suffered the injustice and then were blamed for it.

It seems to me that if we can imagine the injustice we can imagine its opposite. And we can *have* justice.

I say that for two reasons. I say it because I believe that the great things about Australian social democracy reflect a fundamental belief in justice. And I say it because in so many other areas we have proved our capacity over the years to go on extending the realms of participation, opportunity and care.

Just as Australians living in the relatively narrow and insular Australia of the 1960s imagined a culturally diverse, worldly and open Australia, and in a generation turned the idea into reality, so we can turn the goals of reconciliation into reality.

There are very good signs that the process has begun. The creation of the Reconciliation Council is evidence itself. The establishment of the ATSIC – the Aboriginal and Torres Strait Islander Commission – is also evidence. The Council is the product of imagination and good will.

ATSIC emerges from the vision of indigenous self-determination and self-management. The vision has already become the reality of almost 800 elected Aboriginal Regional Councillors and Commissioners determining priorities and developing their own programs. All over Australia, Aboriginal and Torres Strait Islander communities are taking charge of their own lives. And assistance with the problems which chronically beset them is at last being made available in ways developed by the communities themselves.

If these things offer hope, so does the fact that this generation of Australians is better informed about Aboriginal culture and achievement, and about the injustice that has been done, than any generation before. We are beginning to more generally appreciate the depth and the diversity of Aboriginal and Torres Strait Islander cultures. From their music and art and dance we are beginning to recognise how much richer our national life and identity will be for the participation of Aboriginals and Torres Strait Islanders. We are beginning to learn what the indigenous people have known for thousands of years – how to live with our physical environment. Ever so gradually we are learning how to see Australia through Aboriginal eyes, beginning to recognise the wisdom contained in their epic story.

I think we are beginning to see how much we owe the indigenous Australians and how much we have lost by living so apart.

I said we non-indigenous Australians should try to imagine the Aboriginal view. It can't be too hard. Someone imagined this event today, and it is now a marvelous reality and a great reason for hope.

There is one thing today we *cannot* imagine.

We cannot imagine that the descendants of people whose genius and resilience maintained a culture here through fifty thousand years or more, through cataclysmic changes to the climate and environment, and who then survived two centuries of dispossession and abuse, will be denied their place in the modern Australian nation.

We cannot imagine that.

We cannot imagine that we will fail.

And with the spirit that is here today I am confident that we won't.

I am confident that we *will* succeed in this decade.

Thank you.

LITERARY

SPEECHES

PORTIA

In Shakespeare's *The Merchant of Venice* Act IV, Scene I

The Merchant of Venice tells the story of Portia, a wealthy heiress, and her quest to marry her true love, Bassanio. In this scene, Portia, disguised as a young man of law, attempts to save the life of Bassanio's best friend, Antonio, by pleading with his debtor to have mercy.

The quality of mercy is not strained,
It droppeth as the gentle rain from heaven,
Upon the place beneath: it is twice blessed;
It blesseth him that gives and him that takes:
'Tis mightiest in the mightiest; it becomes
The throned monarch better than his crown;
His sceptre shows the force of temporal power,
The attribute to awe and majesty,
Wherein doth sit the dread and fear of kings;
But mercy is above this sceptred sway,
It is enthroned in the hearts of kings,
It is an attribute to God himself,
And earthly power doth then show likest God's
When mercy seasons justice. Therefore, Jew,
Though justice be thy plea, consider this,
That in the course of justice none of us
Should see salvation: we do pray for mercy,
And that same prayer doth teach us all to render
The deeds of mercy.

ROMEO

Shakespeare's famous Romeo and Juliet *is a tragic tale of romance. In this oft-quoted soliloquy, Romeo is enchanted by Juliet's beauty when he sees her appear at the window.*

But, soft! What light through yonder window breaks?
It is the east, and Juliet is the sun!
Arise, fair sun, and kill the envious moon,
Who is already sick and pale with grief,
That though her maid art far more fair than she:
Be not her maid, since she is envious;
Her vestal livery is but sick and green,
And none but fools do wear it; cast it off.
It is my lady; O! it is my love:
O! that she knew she were.
She speaks, yet she says nothing: what of that?
Her eye discourse; I will answer it.
I am too bold, 'tis not to me she speaks:
Two of the fairest stars in all the heaven,
Having some business, do entreat her eyes
To twinkle in their spheres till they return.
What if her eyes were there, they in her head?
The brightness of her cheek would shame those stars
As daylight doth a lamp; her eyes in heaven
Would through the airy region stream so bright
That birds would sing and think it were not night.
See! how she leans her cheek upon that hand,
O! that I were a glove upon that hand,
That I might touch that cheek.

RICHARD III
In Shakespeare's *Richard III* Act I, Scene I

In Richard III, *Richard, the younger brother of King Edward IV, conspires to win the throne by any means necessary. In this opening scene, Richard explains that after a lengthy civil war, peace has at last returned, Edward has the throne, and all of England is rejoicing. Bitter that he was born deformed and ugly, Richard envisages his own treachery and vows to spread misery to everyone around him.*

Now is the winter of our discontent
Made glorious summer by this son of York;
And all the clouds that lowered upon our house
In the deep bosom of the ocean buried.
Now are our brows bound with victorious wreaths,
Our bruised arms hung up for monuments,
Our stern alarums changed to merry meetings,
Our dreadful marches to delightful measures.
Grim-visaged war hath smoothed his wrinkled front,
And now, instead of mounting barbed steeds,
To fright the souls of fearful adversaries,
He capers nimbly in a lady's chamber
To the lascivious pleasing of a lute.
But I, that am not shaped for sportive tricks,
Nor made to court an amorous looking-glass;
I, that am rudely stamped, and want love's majesty
To strut before a wanton ambling nymph;
I, that am curtailed of this fair proportion,
Cheated of feature by dissembling Nature,
Deformed, unfinished, sent before my time

Into this breathing world scarce half made up,
And that so lamely and unfashionable
That dogs bark at me as I halt by them –
Why I, in this weak piping time of peace,
Have no delight to pass away the time,
Unless to spy my shadow in the sun
And descant on mine own deformity.
And therefore, since I cannot prove a lover
To entertain these fair well-spoken days,
I am determined to prove a villain
And hate the idle pleasures of these days.
Plots have I laid, inductions dangerous,
By drunken prophecies, libels, and dreams,
To set my brother Clarence and the King
In deadly hate the one against the other;
And if King Edward be as true and just
As I am subtle, false, and treacherous,
This day should Clarence closely be mewed up
About a prophecy which says that G
Of Edward's heirs the murderer shall be.

MARC ANTONY

In Shakespeare's *Julius Caesar* Act III, Scene II

Julius Caesar tells the story of the murder of Caesar,
plotted and carried out by his friends Brutus and Cassius.
This funeral oration is given by Antony, his true friend,
who urges the crowd to revolt against the conspirators.

Friends, Romans, countrymen, lend me your ears;
I come to bury Caesar, not to praise him.
The evil that men do lives after them;
The good is oft interred with their bones;
So let it be with Caesar. The noble Brutus
Hath told you Caesar was ambitious:
If it were so, it was a grievous fault,
And grievously hath Caesar answered it.
Here, under leave of Brutus and the rest,
For Brutus is an honourable man;
So are they all, all honourable men;
Come I to speak in Caesar's funeral.
He was my friend, faithful and just to me:
But Brutus says he was ambitious;
And Brutus is an honourable man.
He hath brought many captives home to Rome,
Whose ransoms did the general coffers fill:
Did this in Caesar seem ambitious?
When that the poor have cried, Caesar hath wept:
Ambition should be made of sterner stuff:
Yet Brutus says he was ambitious;
And Brutus is an honourable man.
You all did see that on the Lupercal

I thrice presented him a kingly crown
Which he did thrice refuse: was this ambition?
Yet Brutus says he was ambitious;
And, sure, he is an honourable man.
I speak not to disprove what Brutus spoke,
But here I am to speak what I do know.
You all did love him once, not without cause:
What cause withholds you then to mourn for him?
O judgment! thou are fled to brutish beasts,
And men have lost their reason. Bear with me;
My heart is in the coffin there with Caesar,
And I must pause till it come back to me.

AIAS
In Sophocles' *Aias* (*Ajax*)

Sophocles' tragic play Aias (Ajax) *tells the story of Greek hero Aias, who was thought to be second only to Achilles in strength and skill as a warrior. In the play, Aias is consumed by a vengeful passion when the armour of the slain Achilles is awarded not to himself, but to Odysseus.*

The long unmeasured pulse of time moves everything.
There is nothing hidden that it cannot bring to light,
Nothing once known that may not become unknown.
Nothing is impossible. The most sacred oath
Is infallible; a will of iron may bend.
A little while ago, I was tough-tempered
As the hardest iron; but now my edge is blunted
By a woman's soft persuasion. I am loth
To leave a widow and a fatherless child
Here among enemies. This is what I must do:
I must go to the meadows by the sea
And wash till I am clean of all this filth,
So that the Goddess may withhold her wrath
And spare me. I will take this sword of mine,
My adversary, to some secret place
And hide it, bury it out of sight for ever,
Consigned to death and darkness. It was Hector's
My deadliest enemy's gift, and since I had it
The Greeks have done me nothing but ill. How true
The saying is, it is always dangerous
To touch an enemy's gifts. I have learned my lesson,
To obey the gods – and not be disrespectful

To the sons of Atreus; they are in command,
And we are under them; that is as it should be.
There is no power so sacred, none so strong
As to defy all rank and precedence.
The snowy feet of Winter walk away
Before ripe Summer; and patrolling Night
Breaks off her rounds to let the Dawn ride in
On silver horses lighting up the sky.
The winds abate and leave the groaning sea
To sleep awhile. Even omnipotent Sleep
Locks and unlocks his doors and cannot hold
His prisoners bound for ever. Must not we
Learn this self-discipline? I think we must.
I now know this, that while I hate my enemy
I must remember that the time may come
When he will be my friend; as, loving my friend
And doing him service, I shall not forget
That he one day may be my enemy.
Friendship is but a treacherous anchorage,
As most men know . . . Well, never mind . . .
Tecmessa,
You must go in, and ask the blessed gods
To grant me all my heart's desire. (She goes.)
And you,
My friends, to help me, join your prayers with hers.
Ask Teucer, when he comes, to see to things
As I would wish, and to look after you.
Do this for me. I must be on my way.
When next you hear of me, I shall be safe,
And all this suffering ended.

HENRY V
In Shakespeare's *Henry V* Act III, Scene I

In Henry V, *King Henry V decides to invade France in order to take possession of certain lands he claims belong to England. Henry gives this impassioned motivational speech as his men prepare to storm the French town of Harfleur, inspiring the soldiers to victory in battle. They win the fight against all odds.*

Once more unto the breach, dear friends, once more;
Or close the wall up with our English dead!
In peace there's nothing so becomes a man
As modest stillness and humility:
But when the blast of war blows in our ears,
Then imitate the action of the tiger;
Stiffen the sinews, summon up the blood,
Disguise fair nature with hard-favoured rage;
Then lend the eye a terrible aspect;
Let it pry through the portage of the head
Like the brass cannon; let the brow overwhelm it
As fearfully as doth a galled rock
Overhang and jutty his confounded base,
Swilled with the wild and wasteful ocean.
Now set the teeth and stretch the nostril wide,
Hold hard the breath, and bend up every spirit
To his full height! On, on, you noblest English!
Whose blood is fet from fathers of war-proof;
Fathers that, like so many Alexanders,
Have in these parts from morn till even fought,
And sheathed their swords for lack of argument.

Dishonour not your mothers; now attest
That those whom you called fathers did beget you.
Be copy now to men of grosser blood,
And teach them how to war. And you, good yeoman,
Whose limbs were made in England, show us here
The mettle of your pasture; let us swear
That you are worth your breeding; which I doubt not;
For there is none of you so mean and base
That hath not noble lustre in your eyes.
I see you stand like greyhounds in the slips;
Straining upon the start. The game's afoot:
Follow your spirit; and, upon this charge
Cry 'God for Harry, England and Saint George!'

ACKNOWLEDGEMENTS

The publisher wishes to thank copyright holders for permission to reproduce the following material:

Paul Keating. Speech by the Hon. Prime Minister, P.J. Keating MP, Australian Launch of the International Year for the World's Indigenous People, Redfern, 10 December 1992, Prime Minister's Department. © Commonwealth of Australia reproduced by permission.

Martin Luther King. Reprinted by arrangement with the Estate of Martin Luther King Jr., c/o Writers House as agent for the proprietor New York, NY. © 1963 Martin Luther King Jr, copyright renewed 1991 Coretta Scott King.

Nelson Mandela. From *Higher than Hope: The Authorised Biography*, by Fatima Meer (Hamish Hamilton, 1990). © Fatima Meer, 1990. Reproduced for US distribution by permission of Sheil Land Associates Ltd. Reproduced for distribution throughout the Commonwealth, Europe and Canada by permission of Penguin Books Ltd.

Sophocles' *Aias (Ajax)*. From *Electra and Other Plays*, by Sophocles, translated by E.F. Watling (Penguin Classics, 1947) © E. F. Watling, 1947, 1974. Reprinted with permission of Penguin Books Ltd.

Gough Whitlam. 'Handback of Gurindji Lands', from *The Whitlam Government 1972–1975*, by Gough Whitlam. Reprinted by permission of The Honourable Gough Whitlam.

Gough Whitlam. 'Well May We Say "God Save the Queen"', from *The Truth of the Matter*, by Gough Whitlam. Reprinted by permission of The Honourable Gough Whitlam.

Every effort has been made by the editors and publisher to trace and acknowledge copyright material. The publisher would be pleased to hear from any copyright holders who have not been acknowledged.